ARTIST SURVIVAL SKILLS

How to Make a Living as a Canadian Visual Artist

CHRISTOPHER TYRELL

C.T. Productions
Vancouver

Published by C.T. Productions
c/o London Place
#707 – 1177 Hornby Street
Vancouver, British Columbia, Canada
V6Z 2E9
artistsurvivalskills.com

Library and Archives Canada Cataloguing in Publication

Tyrell, Chris, 1947-
Artist survival skills : how to make a living as a Canadian visual artist / by Chris Tyrell.

Includes index.

ISBN 978-0-9809528-0-3

1. Art—Marketing. 2. Art—Economic aspects. 3. Art—Vocational guidance—Canada. I. Title.

N6545.6 T97 2008 706′.8 C2008-902634-9

Editing by: Bethanne Grabham
Design by: Vancouver Desktop Publishing
Cover design by: Stephen O. Schilling

To my friends Beth, Bruce, and Steve, and especially David van Berckel, without whose life-long support this book would not exist.

I am grateful for the assistance of Scott Cronshaw, John Moir, Kitty Blandy, Jane Irwin, Dwight Koss, Stephen Schilling, Patty Osborne, and Bethanne Grabham in the development of this primer.

Contents

Foreword

"Nothing is more common than
unsuccessful men of talent."
— *Calvin Coolidge*

This book has been developed for two reasons: (1) Success in the visual arts, no matter how you define it, comes more readily to artists who manage their careers professionally. (2) There is a particular knowledge deficit in the community of Canadian visual artists concerning the techniques of pricing, promotion, marketing, and sales.

On Success

I have never heard an artist say, "I wish I earned less money from my art." However, after every one of my workshops for artists on ways to increase income, I see expressions of despair on some faces. "I don't like thinking about my art like a business," says one. "Oh my god, I couldn't possibly take all that on," says another, "I'm going to get a gallery to do all that for me."

"Then make art for enjoyment, keep your job, and stop thinking about making more money from your art," I say. This primer is for artists who want to make a career of their creative skills. It addresses art-making in the context of self-employment; it uses business language and subscribes to principles of small business development applicable to any small manufacturing business.

This primer reveals how much work it takes to develop an artistic career. Starting a small business (and this is what we do when we set out to be self-employed artists who sell our work) is a serious challenge regardless of the nature of the business. And while there are many worthwhile books for

Canadian entrepreneurs on starting and growing a small business, this primer looks at key components of small business theory and discusses them in the context of a creative, skills-based small business—the self-employed Canadian visual artist.

Professional Support

There are many associations that support professional artists in Canada. The writers have the Writers Union of Canada, actors, stage managers, and dancers have the Canadian Actors Equity Association and ACRTA; musicians have the Musicians Union. Directors, choreographers, and composers—all artistic professions in Canada have a trade association or union to which they belong. These professional organizations provide support to their members in areas such as health, taxation, and copyrights, and they negotiate collective agreements with employer associations that cover salaries and benefits.

Visual artists, however, do not have sufficient professional guidance and support. Canadian visual artists have Canadian Artists Representation/Front des artists canadiennes (CARFAC) to support them, but only a small percentage of Canadian visual artists are members, so the strength and relevance of the organization is limited. CARFAC and its Copyright Collective are important resources for Canadian visual artists. Many of the issues dealt with in this primer are also the concern of CARFAC, so the organization has developed a large inventory of advisory notes for Canadian visual artists (*see Appendix A for a complete listing.*) (One dollar from each sale of this primer is donated to CARFAC.)

And although Canadian artists are supported through the resources of other organizations, such as local arts councils, peer associations, non-profit cooperatives, artist collectives and publications, this primer seeks to provide a comprehensive overview of professional development issues for the committed Canadian visual artist.

The Website: artistsurvivalskills.com

The intent of this primer is not to provide the definitive resource for Canadian visual artists. Rather, it is a beginning that can be completed and developed as this primer was, in consultation with visual artists and from their experiences as well as my own. Updates and corrections to the text of this primer plus additional relevant material will be posted on the website *artistsurvivalskills.com.* — *Chris Tyrell, September 2008*

Caveats

1. The artists' names used in this primer are fictional. Each personal story, however, is the true story of one artist or two artists working collaboratively.
2. The primer is British Columbia and Vancouver centric. I have set out to provide information to serve all Canadian artists, but I am proud to use examples from my province and city. Google and other search engines make it easy for artists anywhere in the country to identify resources in their area and online.
3. I, Christopher Tyrell, cannot be held liable for any and all advice offered in this book or for any outcomes resulting from the application of advice provided herein. This book is a compendium of advice designed to be of assistance to visual artists, and not to replace the professional involvement of accountants, lawyers, and marketers in artists' career development.

ONE

Defining Success and Setting Goals

"If only creativity and money could be separated. But it can't, if only because each artist—be he painter, writer, poet, composer—anyone who makes something where nothing was before, provides occupation and profit for so many others . . . each act of artistic creation supports publishers, critics, libraries, galleries, playhouses, concert halls, actors, printers, framers, musicians, usherettes, cleaners, academics, arts councils, the organizers of international cultural exchanges, arts administrators, Ministers for the Arts and so forth—and the weight can seem excessive, the rewards astonishingly little, and society's expectation that the artist will do it for free (or just enough to keep them alive and still producing) for sheer abstract love of form beauty, Art, oh Art." — *Fay Weldon*

"When you are making 'art,' the muse is supreme; when you want to make money, most artists will benefit from paying attention to the marketplace." — *C. T.*

Introduction

Success rarely happens by accident. Success, no matter how you define it, is nearly always the result of good strategic planning and a tremendous amount of painstaking work. As a visual artist who wants to develop a successful artistic career, you should address these strategic elements that will help set yourself on a path toward the achievement your goals:

1. Have both a life plan and a career plan (with defined professional and business goals; as an artist, your career plan is your business plan).
2. Consider your personality as part of marketing—specifically sales and self-promotion.

Life & Career Plans

Time is a commodity that is as important as talent for artists wanting to earn all, most of, or part of their income from the making of art. Time is a commodity, like talent, that must be effectively managed. A life plan cohesively integrates your personal and career objectives. It consists of your (and your family's) personal and professional goals, a long-term and short-term strategy for the achievement of those goals, and projected annual budgets. A life plan helps you manage time, ensuring you have enough of it for your personal/individual needs, your social needs (with family and friends), and your professional needs. A well-developed life plan keeps your personal life and your professional life in balance.

The career plan is part of the life plan and is a development (growth) strategy for your artistic practice. A well-planned career plan takes you, step by step, to the successful attainment of your career goals. A good plan will assist you in effectively managing time for creation, administration, and sales and marketing. And, as with the greater life plan, it will have both long- and short-term measurable objectives and current and projected annual budgets.

At the base of your career plan is your professional goal, or mission, and from it, you derive measurable, progressive objectives for each operational year. Defining your professional goal often requires that you consider what, for you, constitutes success.

The development of good life and career plans requires an investment of considerable thought and time. It often brings about a change in behavior, requiring artists to make a time priority for administration and marketing that matches the time commitment for creating work. Good planning can seem like a daunting task, but it is worth the effort and can give you the motivation, confidence, and conviction you need to achieve your objectives.

Define Success: Set Career Goals

Successful artists take charge of their lives and set goals that are desirable, fulfilling, measurable and realistic. A good definition of success considers both the aesthetic and the practical—expressed clearly and concisely.

Sean is an artist/photographer who attended a career development workshop. As an emerging artist, his professional goal (mission statement) derived at the workshop is: "To be respected for my artistic/creative skills and make $50,000 a year from selling my artwork and creative services."

To evaluate his progress, Sean will set business-oriented objectives:

1. Count his sales and total his sales income.
2. Document all creative service sold and solicit and record client evaluations.
3. Document all his exhibition opportunities and note the reputation of the galleries hosting his exhibitions.
4. Track all sales, grants, and reviews generated by his exhibitions.
5. Review comments in the guest book he leaves in each exhibition space.
6. Seek feedback from the gallery owners and curators where his shows occurred.
7. Research his buyers (did a respected private or corporate collector purchase a work?).

Sean has realistic and achievable goals, a diversified source of income, and he knows what he wants out of life. Sean revealed to workshop participants that he sells enough paintings to keep him happy and he receives income from renting out his studio as well as by doing some teaching at the community centre. Further, he revealed that his wife supports his goal of giving up his construction job in order to become a full-time artist.

Visual art careers are divergent—they range from the architect to the craftsperson whose sole outlet is an annual craft fair, from video artists to photographers, designers to sculptors, and performance artists to installation artists. Some earn an enormous income; others live the cliché of creative poverty.

To generalize and to simplify, there are two models of an artist who has unquestionable success in the visual arts:

1. The artist who achieves critical acclaim, exhibits regularly in not-for-profit public galleries, frequently wins awards, and receives grants from the Canada Council for the Arts (and possibly teaches art in an accredited post-secondary institution).
2. The artist who sells a lot of work, is represented by a commercial or private gallery, and often is a teacher of workshops and courses in non-accredited educational environments.

Example: Rachel, part 1

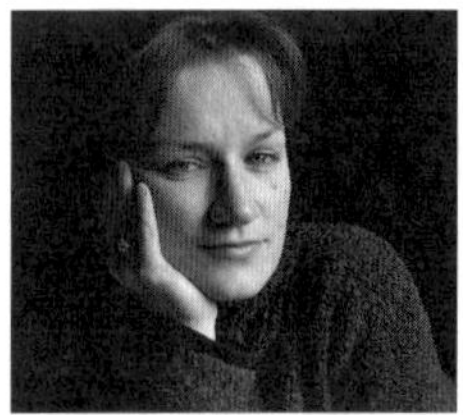

Rachel, an artist who recently graduated with her BFA, attended a workshop on life and career planning for visual art students. There, the facilitator sought to ensure that each participant left with a document summarizing her or his life and career goals made in the session.

This is Rachel's summary, which includes her overall life and career goals and two consecutive five-year objectives that will guide her toward those goals:

1. Life and career goals:

- A career in the visual arts
- To marry and have children
- To have enough family income to provide sufficiently well for the family
- To share in the generation of that income to the best of my ability
- To limit my work to my creative practice
- To be able to take an interesting vacation bi-annually

2. Objectives, post-graduation, first five years:

- Secure a career-related, part-time job
- Secure shared studio space

Sean shares career ambitions that typify many contemporary visual artists who combine elements of both models of success in their mission statement.

Emerging artists should be careful to define success realistically, setting modest initial goals and predicting slow and steady annual growth in a five-year plan. By definition, emerging artists have little experience to draw upon in setting career goals and business plans, whereas seasoned artists have the benefit of experience. Many artists have income derived from non-artistic sources helping to underwrite their creative careers—they may have modest artistic career objectives, as might retirees. With success defined and with realistic, measurable, and achievable goals set, you will be ready to make effective plans for the growth of your artistic practice.

- Establish and maintain an inventory diary
- Establish a price rationale
- Develop a marketable product (line) with integrity
- Develop enough fine art for at least one show a year
- Secure a retail outlet for my product(s)
- Get a gallery to represent my fine art
- Have annual sales from both sources of net revenue of $5000 in three years
- Have annual sales of $10,000 in five years
- Have found Mr Right
- Have objectives for years eleven to fifteen after graduation (and baby number two)

3. Objectives, second five years:

- Quit the part-time job
- Secure commercial product outlets in two other markets
- Have at least two shows outside Vancouver
- Have my own studio attached to the house
- Boost prices and increase sales so that annual net income reaches $20,000
- Have first child
- Have a plan for years sixteen to twenty

Career/Business Planning

A strong career, or business, plan for Sean will involve:

1. Income projections matching his current income plus 15% to cover increased costs.
2. Consistent growth in each operational year.
3. A growth strategy for his existing sources of revenue (or revenue streams): teaching and sales.
4. A development strategy for an additional revenue stream (or two).
5. An advertising/marketing plan to support the desired growth.

Key components of an effective growth strategy in a market economy involve the right pricing, having market-friendly products, and excellent marketing skills. Successful small manufacturing businesses, including those based on creative practice, have business plans that include an accurate and complete sales/inventory index, a carefully rationalized pricing system that includes every type of product, and a detailed marketing strategy for all forms of inventory.

Your banker, successful artist friends, peer associations, and an infinite number of online resources can help you define your business goals and provide you with guidance on the format and scale of business planning that is right for you. Most self-employed artists are likely to find that a simple business plan is all they need.

Personality Issues

There's no easy way to say it: some artists have personalities that reduce their potential for success. Professionals of any field with a chip on their shoulder, or who have victim personalities, are strident, militant, constantly negative, or who have otherwise challenging personalities, can face tremendous challenges in the marketplace. Also, shyness or introversion can, unfortunately, make it hard for the artist to be an effective self-promoter. (People who are introverted may benefit from membership in an art club or society that facilitates group marketing and sales initiatives.) Conversely, extroversion is an asset for the entrepreneurial artist. And listening skills are important—artists must be able to read their customers and potential customers, knowing when to back off and when to move forward. Sales and marketing is a game of relationships and you have to be able to play it.

Confidence is a key factor of success. There is always a way to be confident, you just have to find it. You must be able to express complete confidence in yourself and your work—but that does not mean being a bragging bore. It means modestly expressed, assured confidence; there is nothing like it to convince customers that you are worthy of their investment.

If you are detail-oriented or meticulous in your approach to tasks, it will be of great benefit to your career. The tracking of receipts, cataloging of inventory, bookkeeping, and the management of time is vital to effective self-business development. If your personality works well with these kind of administrative duties, it will make success far more likely. A personality familiar with discipline, adaptability, multi-tasking, and a positive attitude will likely do very well in sales-based creative self-employment.

Getting Help

The degree of variance in lifestyles and expectations amongst artists reading this primer prevents the offering of specific practical tips on the development of your business plan. You will have to do some research and take advantage of the many resources available to entrepreneurs. Your province may have a Ministry or Department of Small Business or Better Business Bureaus, or other business associations may offer courses on starting a small business; all these resources offer detailed and annotated advice on planning. Regional colleges and technical institutes often offer courses in starting a small business that focus on effective plan development. Google "starting a small business" or "business planning" and you will find a treasure of free resources to assist you in developing a business plan. These resources are not art industry specific; you will have to do some interpretation.

Example: Rachel, part II

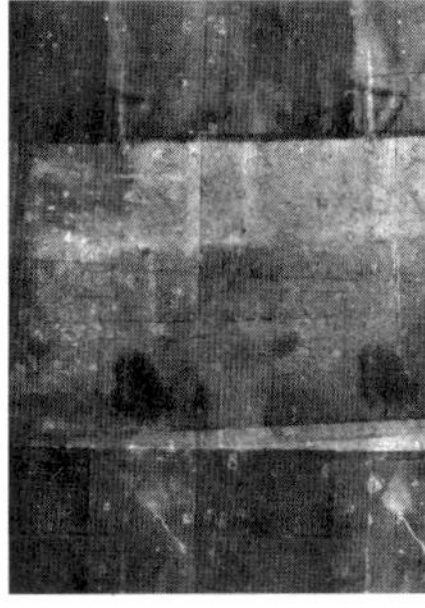

At the workshop, Rachel made a career plan (see below) for her first couple of years. As she is at the very beginning of her artistic career, she has some doubts and fears. She does not want to put undue pressure on herself or leave herself open to failure at an early age. So, she says wisely, she will remain flexible in the first few years of post-graduate, practical working experience; her career plan serves as a guide and gives her measurable goals.

YEAR ONE

1. **Get a career-related job (immediate)**
    - Put together my portfolio
    - Make business cards
    - Write a good CV
    - Get letters from (2 professors and a former employer)
    - Create a mailing list (include all the galleries I want to work for, email friends about me wanting a job and send professional emails to all galleries)
    - Regularly check Alliance for the Arts website job page
    - Go to an opening or two a week, and ask about studio space and work
2. **Create an inventory diary**
    - Enter all my good stuff into the diary
    - Price work like mine
    - Set my prices-per-square-inch for fine art
3. **Get a studio**
    - See if [family friend] will let me use part of his warehouse and if [relative] will let me use their garage
    - Check with everyone from my studio classes to see what they are doing
    - Ask everyone I can at East Side Culture Crawl (for a shared space!)
    - Check out Malaspina Printmakers membership

4. **Research a commercial line**
    - Check out who's selling giclées and at what prices
    - Check out GI Gallery to see what silk screens are going at
    - Check with DB about his agent; GI Gallery that buys designs
    - Apprentice with an illustrator for a few months
    - Talk to [four names were listed] about their commercial lines
5. **Develop fine art practice**
    - Create at least five more pieces for *Myth* series

YEAR TWO

1. **Prepare for getting a show**
    - Increase inventory for *Myth* series to have enough pieces for a show
    - Develop an artist statement for the show
    - Get the best *Myth* images shot for my portfolio
    - Check with [three artists' names] about their galleries (would they recommend me? Could they get me an appointment?)
2. **Develop commercial line for business**
    - Be in production by July
    - Have stock by November
    - Research, choose, and join group for Christmas sale
    - Research retail art outlets for giclées or silk screens
3. **Reconsider part-time work**
    - Assess current position
    - Seek raise (or more or less hours? Get a better paying job?)
4. **Conduct research for career and business development**
    - Check with [artist's name] about residencies
    - Check out MFA programs for following year
    - Check out courses on how to build a website; research server options

TWO

Pricing Your Art

"A fair price is the highest one a collector can be induced to pay."
— *Robert Hughes*

"Pricing your art is one of the most important decisions you face. If there is no cohesive philosophy at the base of your price decision-making, you are putting yourself at risk—the implications of your pricing, donation receipting, and insurance evaluations are enormous."
— *C. T.*

What Is a Price Rationale?

Setting the right price for your artwork is a critical component of business planning. A good pricing strategy ensures that the prices for all the work and services you sell have a relationship to one another. The market ultimately determines the value of your work, but there are many tools available to help you price your artwork effectively. A "price rationale" unifies, in one coherent theory, the pricing of all the divergent art products of your creative practice.

Creating a price rationale involves a number of factors, such as:

1. Recording the dimensions and prices of your past work sold in an inventory diary.
2. Understanding pricing per square inch (or developing an alternative pricing formula).
3. Identifying your artistic level.
4. Researching the prices of works by other artists in your market area who work in similar sizes and media and at your professional level.
5. Understanding when and how to raise prices.
6. Understanding the implications of recording sales on insurance claims.

The Artist's Inventory Diary

A key aspect of professional management for visual artists is record keeping. A record of inventory is the artist's "professional diary"; it is a place to keep all your important business information. A good inventory diary can make bookkeeping and doing your tax returns very easy for you (or for your accountant). You can create your inventory diary in the appropriate software of your choice (likely a database) or on paper in a three-ring binder that allows you to easily add or change pages to any section. The diary has two component parts: an inventory list that grows as you produce work and a concurrent section that includes pricing calculations, sales records, and other notes that list your awards, reviews, and/or publications

By keeping inventory, sales records, and awards and publicity in a diary, book, or list form, you are reminded of the importance of making regular entries. It is a chronologic record and critical professional tool. Every time you produce work, you add it to your inventory list, which includes the title, dimensions, medium, and materials used, creation date, and price(s). You also will record information on the source of the image (if appropriate) and a reference to the location of a photographic record of the work. Every time you sell something, you update its record, adding the sales figure, date of sale, tax charged, and listing any tax paid or collected, et cetera. When you sell your work, it also is a good idea to record the buyer's name and contact information (whenever possible). And somewhere in the list, record all travel expenses legitimately related to the making of your art. Each work you create may be given an inventory number, with your sales records and receipts carrying that inventory number. (This is very effective when, as in the example of Sylvia's inventory list shown in figure 2.1, titles of two or more pieces are similar.)

If you make multiples (e.g., prints, cards, or casts), you record the series as a single entry, as Sylvia has done for her series of seriographs (silk screens), *Mother Watches Me*. If you make multiples of different sizes, each size is one entry in your inventory—again, with the number (volume) of copies also listed.

In summary, each artwork in an inventory diary contains:

1. Name of work or description of work.
2. Product number (optional).
3. Date of completion.
4. Dimensions.
5. List of materials used.
6. Location of the item's photographic record (always photo-document your work).
7. Price: retail and wholesale.
8. Location (e.g., studio, gallery, or home of a friend).
9. Current status (e.g., sold, on consignment, on loan, rented).
10. Sale information (include location, date, and amount).
11. Tax (e.g., collected, paid, or owing).

Sylvia's Record Keeping

Sylvia is a painter who lives in Vancouver. She produces ten to twelve canvases each year and she selects two or three of each year's works for reproduction as

Name or Description and Materials	Prod. #	Vol. #	Date Made	Dimensions W X H	Slide/ Image #	Price		Location	Status	Revenue Received	Sale Date	Sales tax	GST
						Retail	Wholesale						
Mother Protects Me Pencil crayon, graphite, gold leaf, mylar	46	1	Feb. 06	20" X 16"	Slide #51	$460	$230	Burrows Gallery	Consigned				
Mother Protects Me II Pencil crayon, graphite, gold leaf	47	1	Mar. 06	20" X 16"	Slide #52	$460	$230 (Law Firm)	Cameron Driege	Sold	$230	Oct 06 Burrows	Paid by Burrows	Paid by
Mother Watches Me (ORIGINAL) Pencil crayon, graphite, gold leaf	48	1	Mar. 06	16" X 12"	Slide #53	$275	$140	Home of Mrs. L. Burrows	Sold	$140	Oct 06	Paid by Burrows	Paid by Burrows
Is She Looking? Graphite on hand-made paper	49	1	Apr. 06	12" X 18"	Slide #54	$175	$90	Burrows Gallery	Consigned				
She Sees Me Graphite on hand-made paper	50	1	Apr. 06	18" X 12"	Slide #55	$175	$90	Marie Lachance	Sold	$175	May 06	12.25	10.50
She Can't See Me Here Pencil crayon, graphite, on hand-made paper	51	1	Apr. 06	18" X 12"	Slide #56	$175	$90	Burrows Gallery	Consigned				
Will She Find Me? Pencil crayon, graphite, on hand-made paper	52	1	Apr. 06	18" X 12"	Slide #57	$175	$90	Burrows Gallery	Consigned				
She Can See Me! Pencil crayon, graphite, on hand-made paper	53	1	Apr. 06	18" X 12"	Slide #58	$175	$90	Burrows Gallery	Consigned				
Mother Watches Me (PRINTS)													
Seriographs (black)	54	20	May. 06	12" X 8"	Slide #59	$100	$50	Burrows Gallery	9 sold	$450	Oct 06	BG Paid	BG Paid
Seriographs (sepia)	55	20	May. 06	12" X 8"	Slide #60	$100	$50	Burrows Gallery	13 sold	$650	Oct 06	BG Paid	BG Paid
Can She See Me? Graphite on hand-made paper	56	1	May. 06	20" X 16"	Slide #61	$460	$230	Burrows Gallery	Consigned				
Portrait of Doom Acrylic Painting	57	1	Jun. 06	20" X 40"	Slide #62	$1,200	$600	Burrows Gallery	Consigned				
Maybe She Will Find Me Pencil crayon, graphite, on hand-made paper	58	1	July. 06	20" X 16"	Slide #63	$460	$230	Office of Damon Wilde	Sold	$230	Oct 06	BG Paid	BG Paid
She Found Me Pencil crayon, graphite, on hand-made paper	59	1	July. 06	20" X 16"	Slide #64	$460	$230	Burrows Gallery	Consigned				

Figure 2.1. Sylvia's inventory list

limited edition prints, producing up to 200 editions of each design. She also produces cards that she wholesales in packages of six, or as singles to the same outlets that carry her prints. Her inventory list includes each painting and a single entry for each of her card and print editions. It also allows her to record the number of packages, prints, and single cards when she is producing multiples.

There is a relationship between the prices of her oils and the prices of her prints. Her pricing for her cards is based on what the market will bear, not on creation time and/or the cost of materials. Sylvia monitors market pricing of works similar in medium and size to her work at several galleries in Vancouver. She also sells direct, through her website, to individual buyers across Canada (including relatives, friends, and clients met as a result of her teaching and traveling), which allows her to earn the full retail price on each sale. (*Many galleries do not tolerate this practice. See chapter three about representation.*) Whenever she sells in Vancouver, either through her dealer or on consignment through galleries in other markets, she earns only wholesale prices.

Sylvia's inventory list is a simple model—very few inventory items and very simple pricing: she offers no discounts or bulk sales prices. Artists with a wider variety of products and services that sell at retail, wholesale, and at other discount prices, require a more complex recording system. All record keeping, especially for artists with complex inventory, is best done on an electronic database. Spreadsheet programs (such as Excel or Filemaker Pro) make inventory tracking and sales recording very easy to manage.

Mark's Record Keeping

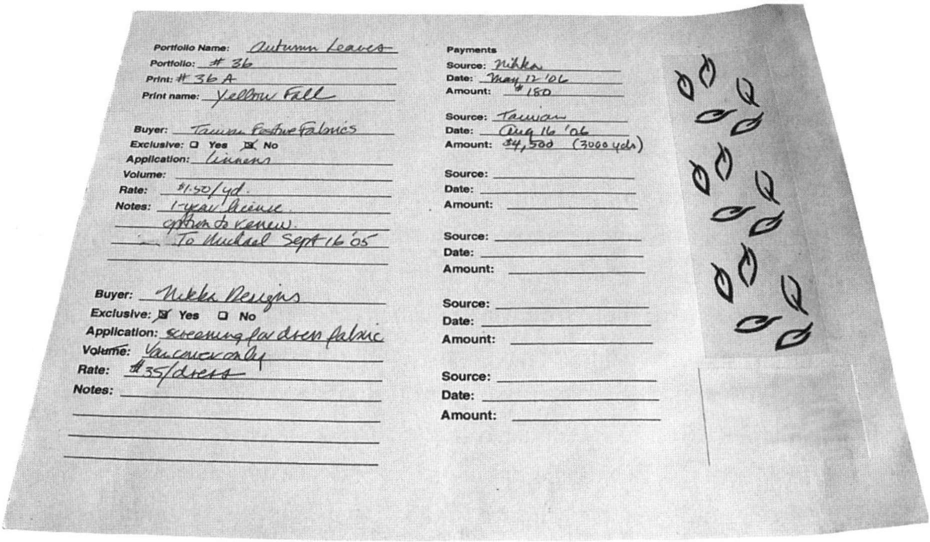

Figure 2.2. Mark's inventory book

Mark makes monoprints on paper. Monoprinting is an practice that combines aspects of printmaking (producing multiples) and painting (producing individual original works). He produces a series of ten-to-fifteen single images that relate very strongly to each other and he makes several such series for his annual exhibitions. His designs also go to an agent who brokers his work to publishers. Mark's inventory diary is a book that contains a page for each work bearing a sample image of the design (see figure 2.2). As his agent sells his designs that lead to the production of items, he adds the derivative products as items in his inventory book. If, as happened to Mark, Ikea buys one of his images to print and sell as a poster, he lists the poster as an item on the inventory list, bearing the design used in the poster, and then records all revenue earned from its sales. Every product manufactured from this design becomes a revenue stream and is added to his inventory book.

Because of Mark's own unique situation, he has created a system for his record keeping that is appropriate for the work he does. That is what each artist must do: find the right system and medium for keeping all your records.

Know Your Artistic Level

Objectively identifying your artistic/career level is important for your comparative pricing research. Perhaps you self-identify as an amateur or recreational artist; perhaps you think of yourself as a professional. Although the word "amateur" can feel like an artistic dismissal to some, an amateur artist is simply someone who derives pleasure from the making of art, but who earns the majority of his or her income from sources other than the sale of art. Amateurs make art for the love of the process, as a hobby, and should price low.

When the adjective "professional" is applied to visual artists, it usually describes either the their approach to their career management, or it describes artists with commercial representation and a decent history of shows and sales. Professionals can be at the beginning stages of their career, mid-career or accomplished. Regardless of their level, professional artists must price appropriately, at the maximum the market will bear.

If you are unclear about your career level, you can consult community resources for help. Local art club members, public non-profit gallery programmers or curators, post-secondary art teachers, and owners of commercial art galleries can all help you to properly identify peer artists in your market area.

Price per Square Inch

A price-per-square-inch pricing system can sound too industrial or commercial to some artists at first, but it is a logical and proven method that guarantees price coherence and stability throughout a career as well as ongoing customer satisfaction. To calculate the price-per-square-inch of a work of art is simple: multiply the length of the piece by its width to get the number of square inches, and then divide the price of the piece by the number of square inches:

Width × height = the number of square inches

(Retail or full) Price ÷ number of square inches = price-per-square-inch

Pricing per square inch does not work for sculpture, installation work, video, and film. Artists using these media or who do not like the price-per-square-inch formula must develop their own coherent rationale—one which must protect themselves and their "investors" (buyers) if they are to create a business that lasts.

Price Research

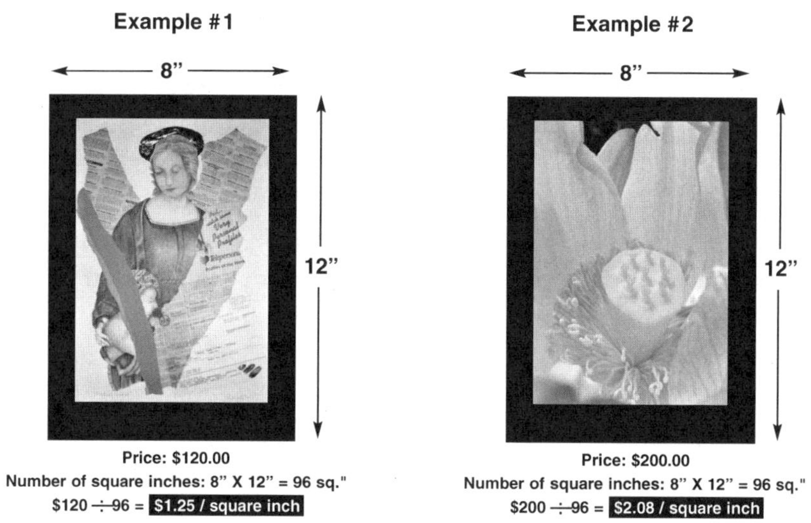

Figure 2.3. In Example #1, the artwork is 8 by 12 inches. It has 96 (8 × 12) square inches, and is for sale at $120. To calculate its price-per-square-inch, 120 is divided by 96 to yield the price-per-square-inch of $1.25. In Example #2, the price of the painting is $200, so the price-per-square-inch is $2.08 ($200 ÷ 96).

To bring order to your pricing—or, to rationalize your pricing system— start by entering the dimensions and prices from past sales into the pricing section of your inventory diary. Next, record the dimensions and prices of works of similar sizes and media done by the artists that match your level of professionalism and who sell in your market area. Calculate the prices-per-square-inch for many of your own works as well as those researched.

As with many things, pricing research can be enjoyable if it is done in the company of another artist. Ask a fellow artist to join you while you do your research at local galleries. Alone or in partnership, by investigating the price-per-square-inch systems of other artists, you become knowledgeable about your market area and you can price your work more effectively.

***An important note*:** When you are doing pricing research, be sure to compare apples with apples. All your research should be based on framed work or unframed work. Price your work framed and unframed, if you need to, in order to be comparing equivalencies.

Susan's Pricing Research

Susan, an artist who works in coloured pencils, conducted pricing research, first on her own past work and then on the work of two other artists with whom she graduated from the Emily Carr Institute of Art and Design in Vancouver: Damian and Matsuko. Damian's prices-per-square-inch (see figure 2.4) are varied in each medium. He clearly has no rationale to his pricing and probably uses a time calculation or his pricing is arbitrary.

Matsuko's pricing (see figure 2.5) is clearly more rationalized than Damian's pricing.

Pricing Research

Artist	Medium	Size	# Sq. Inches	Price	Price/Square Inch
Damian					
Vatican Series '98	Coloured pencil	20 X 24	480	$550	1.14
Vatican Series '98	Coloured pencil	14 X 16	224	$225	1.01
Vatican Series '98	Conté	16 X 20	320	$200	.60
Meridien	Coloured Pencil	16 X 20	320	$800	2.50
Aquifer	Coloured Pencil	16 X 20	320	$650	2.03
Sylvie 2006	Graphite	20 X 40	800	$800	1.00
Syblil Series	Coloured pencil	20 X 24	480	$625	1.30
Mother Series	Coloured Pencil	20 X 16	320	$460	1.43
Mt. Lehman	Graphite	20 X 40	600	$800	1.33
Turniquet	Graphite	16 X 20	320	$800	2.50
Whirlpool	Conté	14 X 16	224	$200	.89
Epiphany	Conté	16 X 20	320	$180	.56

Average PPSI-Graphite: $1.61/ sq."
Average PPSI-Conté: $0.68/ sq."
Average PPSI-Coloured Pencil: $1.56/ sq."
Average PPSI all work: $1.28/ sq."

Figure 2.4. Susan's pricing research on Damian's work

Artist	Medium	Size	# Sq. Inches	Price	Price/Square Inch
Matsuko					
Desoto	Graphite	12 X 18	216	$250	1.15
Cadillac	Graphite	12 X 16	192	$225	1.17
Edsel	Graphite	14 X 20	280	$325	1.16
Northwest Landscape	Graphite	14 X 16	224	$260	1.16
Southern Exposure	Conté + ink	12 X 16	192	$375	1.95
Dantés Landing	Conté + ink	16 X 20	320	$600	1.87
Northwoods	Conté + ink	12 X 18	216	$400	1.85
Pine Beetles	Conté + ink	14 X 20	280	$500	1.78

Pricing Research

Average PPSI-Graphite: $1.16/sq."

Average PPSI-Conté: $1.86/sq."

Average PPSI all work: $1.51/sq."

Figure 2.5. Susan's pricing research on Matsuko's work

Robert Ashcroft's FCA Research

In 2001, Federation of Canadian Artist (FCA) member Robert Ashcroft undertook some comparative pricing research, similar to what you can do. His work was published in *Art Avenues*, the magazine of the FCA (vol. 1, no. 3 [Sept./Oct. 2001], pg.10). In his article, he analyzed the pricing of FCA member artworks pictured in the monthly FCA magazine. (The many works reproduced in each issue are captioned with the artist's name, date of completion, prices, dimensions, and media.)

Ashcroft's study was a quantitative evaluation of pricing. He determined the price-per-square-inch value of each piece based on the ninety-three artworks reproduced in the magazine done by thirty-four different artists. His research revealed average prices-per-square-inch as follows: oils, $3.18 per square inch; acrylics, $3.32 per square inch; and water media, $4.48 per square inch.

Nineteen artists had more than one work in the research inventory and were, therefore, evaluated for consistency in their pricing. Of the nineteen, only seven appeared to be using a rationalized pricing system.

(The FCA is a very professionally run organization. Their members are professional in their approach to their careers. Many have vibrant careers that include several revenue streams; some are master artists and marketers. Ashcroft's figures provide a snapshot view of market pricing for artists of considerable experience and sophistication in the current dollars of the 2001 Vancouver market.)

The Pricing Bee

One great way to do pricing research that is fun and leads to all kinds of other benefits is to organize a "pricing bee." Pricing bees work best when

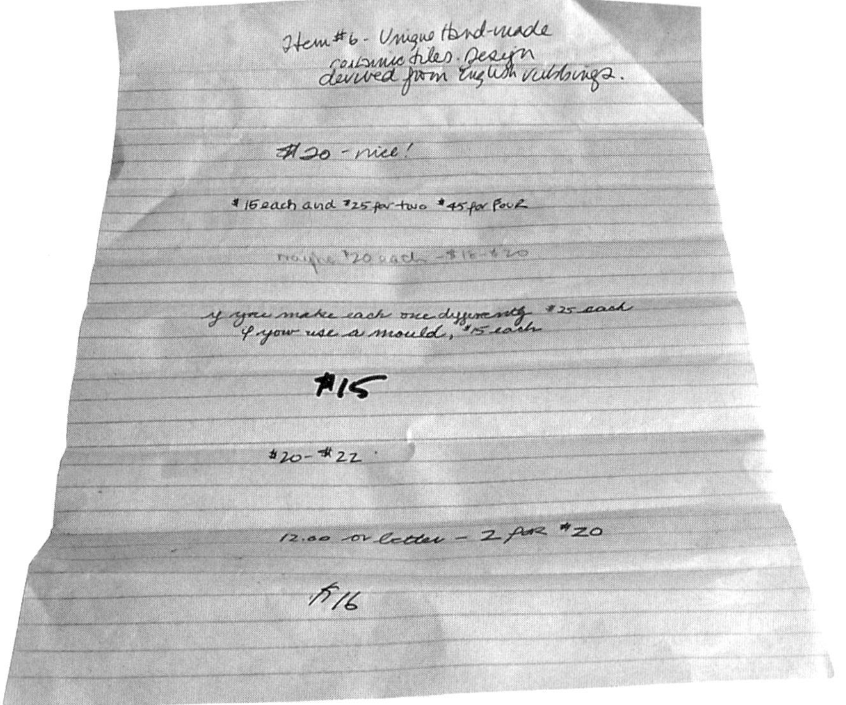

Item #6 - Unique Hand-made ceramic tiles. Design derived from English rubbings.

$20 - nice!

$15 each and $25 for two $45 for Four

maybe $20 each - $18-$20

if you make each one differently $25 each
if you use a mould, $15 each

$15

$20-$22

12.00 or better - 2 for $20

$16

Figure 2.6. Pricing sheet from a pricing bee

several artists participate. Each artist attending the bee brings examples of the various types of inventory items that they plan to offer for sale. Pricing bees are generally held in a room of tables on which participating artists can place the examples of their work, and beside each piece, its maker places a blank piece of paper (or two, depending on the number of participants). Then, when all the work is in place, the participants visit each table and write down on each piece of paper what they would be willing to pay for the corresponding artwork. After the appraisal is written down, the participant folds the paper to conceal the estimate—doing this prevents subsequent appraisers from being influenced by a previous price estimate. At the end of the bee, each participating artist has a sheet of objective estimations of the retail value of his or her work. By adding up the estimates on each sheet of paper and then dividing that number by the number of estimates on the sheet, artists get an average estimated price for each of their appraised pieces.

Figure 2.6 shows a pricing sheet from a pricing bee for a "unique hand-made ceramic tile." There are eight appraisals: $20, $15, $20, $15, $15, $20, and $12. The total of the eight evaluations is $117. To get the average value, $117 is divided by 8. The average value bee participants would therefore pay for one tile is $14.54.

Setting Your Prices

Once you have done all your research, you are ready to set your prices for all the forms of work that you produce. When you establish your pricing rationale, it is best to set base prices for work of different sizes and of different media. Once these values are established, for the rest of your career, price management is very easy: all there is to do is to record inventory once it is produced, price it, and track it until it is sold. Document any temporary or permanent adjustments to your prices-per-square-inch, explaining, in each case, why you made the adjustment.

Artist	Medium	Average Price/Square Inch
My work 2001-2008	Coloured Pencil	1.07
My work 2001-2008	Graphite	.64
Damian	Graphite	1.61
Damian	Conté	.68
Damian	Coloured Pencil	1.56
Matsuko	Graphite	1.16
Matsuko	Conté	1.86
Average 2008 PPSI	Graphite	1.13
Average 2008 PPSI	Conté	1.27
Average 2008 PPSI	Coloured Pencil	1.31

Figure 2.7. Susan's pricing research: comparing her price-per-square-inch to Damian's and Matsuko's

Susan averaged her own past prices plus the prices of two peer artists. These average prices helped her establish a base price for her work in coloured pencils and graphite. She then added 15% to these average prices to establish her base prices of $1.46 per square inch for her works in conté crayon, and $1.50 per square inch for her works in coloured pencil. She set this above-average price base because of her perception of her career position vis-à-vis Damian and Matsuko.

Wholesale Pricing

The wholesale price of your work is the price paid to you by re-sellers, such as an art dealer, gallery, or retail store. It is, therefore, the revenue you receive from a re-seller after its commission has been deducted from the sale of your work. When artists wholesale their work, however, their projected income can be reduced by half if a gallery's sales commission is fifty percent, which is the standard rate. Taking on representation also can mean that artists must then *double their sales* simply to keep their sales income at pre-representation levels. (Or, the artist has to considerably raise her or his prices.)

Selling work at "wholesale prices" (e.g., a 50% discount) is generally effective for close relatives and friends to whom you want to offer price reductions. Also, some artists "grandfather" certain buyers with special pricing, freeze prices at a certain price-per-square-inch level for friends, or give relatives a favoured buyer status. (Be sure to read about the potential impact of price reductions in the Price Rationale & Insurance section below if you make any such special sales. Also, make a note of all these "deals" and why you made them in your inventory diary.)

Increasing Prices

An important part of your inventory diary is tracking milestone events such as awards, grants, appearances in major media or in prestige publications, and/or major sales or commissions. Not on every occasion, but certainly with years in between, these major career events become the justification for an increase in your prices-per-square-inch for all your work (except for things such as cards or other "low end" products that have prices sensitive to those of competitors in your market area). When you decide to raise prices, record the increase and date in your diary, calculating the price

Example: Sophia

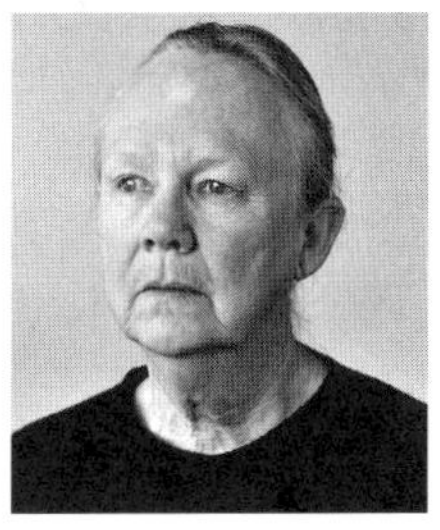

Sophia and her husband are collectors of contemporary art. "My husband and I have decided to build a very strong collection of work that we will donate to a museum," says Sophia. "I've spent the last few years traveling all over the world to art fairs and exhibitions and have a pretty good idea of how the market functions.

"Almost all young artists overprice their work. They need to learn to step back from their emotional investment in their work and be realistic. As a collector, I always consider the artist's exhibition record (especially museum and other curated shows). I am much more confident buying a work for $10,000 if a curator has recognized the artist or if the artist has participated in juried residencies or received grants and awards. I've spoken to many artists who seem to have a sense of entitlement without the credibility to justify their high prices. It's also really important to consider what the market will bear. An artist showing in a respected New York gallery can command higher prices there than in a city like Vancouver."

increases as a percentages of previous prices. It is a simple system, and if a client ever challenges you on a price increase, you will always have a documented response to offer by identifying those milestone career events that accumulated between increases.

Price Rationale & Insurance

It is very important to understand the implications of having a documented and annotated price rationale if you insure your artwork.

If you claim deductions on your income tax for expenses involved in making art, and if you declare your artistic revenues, you are operating as a small business. Your inventory, therefore, is "business inventory." Home insurance policies vary with insurers, but many limit coverage of business inventory. Your insurer may require that you carry "extra" insurance to cover your business inventory if it is in your home. If you have a studio separate from your residence, a separate policy or a separate listing on another policy may be required. Pieces that you place outside your home or studio for sale or exhibition may not be covered by the insurance policy covering your inventory, so you must ensure that the facilities selling or showing your work have insurance policies that can protect your work for the duration of time that it is in their possession and during transportation to and from their space.

Even when you have all the necessary coverage in place, you are not effectively protected if you have a weak or incomplete sales record. Remember that when insurers are selling their policies, they talk in a way that gives naïve listeners the impression that they will be properly compensated for loss, damage, or theft. One doesn't often read the small print at the time of purchase, only to discover complicating caveats when one tries to make a claim on the policy. Insurance claims are readily and quickly processed if you have documentation, such as a police report number in the case of theft, or a notarized statement from the owner of the facility where the theft or damage occurred. But even more important is having a complete annotated sales record.

If you make a claim, your insurer will need to quantify the artistic value of your work in order to compensate you for other than the cost of materials used in making your artwork. "Artistic value" is very hard to prove without documented sales. Your insurer will appropriately compensate you if all your sales are documented. Insurers will pay out to the lowest price-per-square-inch they can justify. If you have the contact information of (recent) buyers of your work, your insurer will be able to verify your sales prices and the price-per-square-inch value of all your work and authorize your claim at the level you expect. If you are asked to provide an insurance company with information from your most recent sales for a claim, you must negotiate that calculations are based on *full retail value*, and not discounted or wholesale prices.

Price Rationale & Taxes

If, in your inventory diary, you record all your career expenses, doing your taxes each year will be easy and you will ensure yourself of maximum deductions. If the Canada Revenue Agency (CRA) audits you, your diary will impress the CRA agent and substantiate all your claims. Having a good professional diary speaks to your professionalism and gives the CRA assurance that your taxes are accurate. (*See chapter twelve.*)

Price Rationale & Donating Art

Federally registered charities can issue tax receipts for artworks donated to them but they require independent valuations. The donor charity is responsible to the Canada Revenue Agency for the valuation of all their in-kind donations. If you make your diary available to the charity employee issuing the tax receipts—specifically your sales record (retail prices!) and price-per-square-inch calculations—and if you can provide contact information for the buyers paying those prices, you can expect that your receipt will be for the value you expect for your work. (*See chapter five.*)

Example: Paul

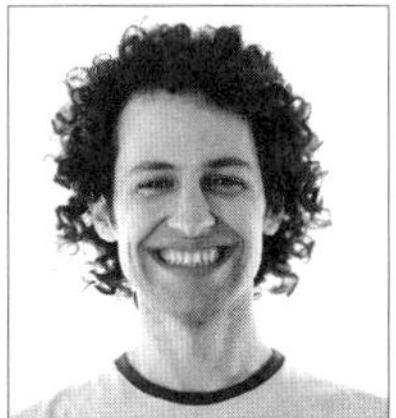

Paul is an accountant. "My experience with artists/clients, including very successful ones," says Paul, "is that none have insured their work other than in transit. I enquired years ago about insurance, and the insurer called it 'listed' property and required a detailed report every time a painting moved from one location to another—a real chore! So, I never bothered with insurance except when it was being shipped. I think the rationale or trade-off for all the tracking is the thought that I can always paint another painting."

An important note: Charities asking for a donation of your work may ask you to pay for any appraisal they require. In such a situation, offer your sales records and the contact information of buyers and state your expectation that this is just as acceptable for their evaluation. If they do not, do not donate your work to them.

THREE

Securing Commercial Representation

"The trouble with being poor is that it takes up all of your time."

— *Willem de Kooning*

"Artists whose definition of success involves making a decent living from creative production should never abrogate their role in sales. Represented or not, the artist remains a primary driver of her or his sales. When there is representation, it is a partnership, but artists who are not overburdened by sales should think of themselves as sharing the driver's seat."

— *C. T.*

Considering Representation

Commercial representation for most Canadian visual artists means having an ongoing consignment or representation agreement with a gallery. The gallery acts as the artist's agent, consulting on pricing and marketing and managing the artist's sales in a defined market area, although some galleries offer a lesser degree of influence or advice. Ideally, the artist is represented by several galleries, each in a different market. Each artist/gallery relationship is as different as the personalities involved; the relationship that develops between the artist and gallery will be what the artist makes of it.

The value of a good representation agreement with a gallery is that it requires you, the artist, to consider all possible eventualities that could extend from the consignment of your work to a third party. The trick is to be strong enough to protect your work without being too demanding and formal that you lose the interest of a gallery that might otherwise represent you.

The trick is to be strong enough to protect your work without being too demanding and formal that you lose the interest of a gallery that might otherwise represent you.

Artists considering representation for the first time should understand that representation means vastly increasing your creative output. James, for example, is an artist in Vancouver who creates paintings of various sizes (averaging 16 by 20 inches) and linoprints that are 8 by 12 inches. The average price for his paintings is $800 and the prints average at $250. In 2007, James sold 12 paintings and 20 prints—all to people in his home market. His gross sales last year totaled $14,600. The average sales commission of galleries in Canada is 40% to 50% of gross sales, so if James makes the same amount of sales in his first year of having representation, he will earn only $7,300 (if he pays a 50% commission). In order to maintain his income at the pre-representation level, his volume of sales must double or his prices must vastly increase.

Increasing volume of sales requires that there be an increased production of inventory, but increasing inventory does not necessarily mean more sales. The right gallery for any artist works to double the artist's sales and/or increase the artist's prices so that the artist does not lose income as a result of their collaboration. Gallery owners sometimes assist artists in securing representation in other markets if the artist can produce sufficient inventory for such an initiative.

The Artistic Ego

The arts industry is ego-based. Artists without confidence will generally not do well at independently representing themselves in the visual art marketplace, and they may be ideal candidates for gallery representation for that reason. Artists with confidence (justified, or not; proportionate to talent, or not) and with gallery representation tend to sell well; they are effective partners for their galleries. Confident, social people make good sales persons as do people of extraordinary talent.

Artists' whose definition of success involves making a decent living from creative production should never abrogate her or his role in sales. Represented or not, artists remain the primary driver of their sales. When there is representation, it is a partnership, but artists who are not overburdened by sales should think of themselves as sharing "the driver's seat." Being represented by a gallery has nothing to do with validation, and in most cases, it is not about having shows and being seen. It is about sales, and representation functions as only a part of the artists' sales plan. The gallery, don't forget, needs to make sales to pay its bills—you are only one of its many clients.

Not all galleries are alike. Some set an excellent model of partnership with the artist; some are disreputable. It all depends on the owner/operator and staff. That is why being selective and interviewing the gallery (as they interview you) is so important.

Choosing a Gallery

Choosing who will represent you is like choosing a spouse. Ideally, the relationship will be mutually beneficial, last a long time, and be free of conflict.

Galleries sometimes have a specialty—such as prints, sculpture, or photography—or they may be focused on representing types of artists—such as established, emerging, or alternative artists. Also, in larger cities, there are often artist collectives, non-profit galleries, and/or community galleries with specific curatorial mandates that can be of interest to artists who sell their work. In communities where there are a lot of galleries, artists can often have a choice of galleries to approach that have a compatible exhibition history or a trustworthy proprietor.

If you have a choice of galleries, the recommendations of peers can help you make your decision. Pay attention to galleries that represent the artists of interest to you, and visit, call, or write to them about management and sales practices at their venue. Ask them how good their sales have been, if there have been any problems, and, if so, how the problems were resolved. Ask about the promptness of payments, and how straightforward the overall artist-gallery relationship is. Another good test of a gallery director is to call him or her a day or two after your interview to see if he or she takes your call and/or how long it takes for him or her to call you back. This is often a good indicator of how you will be treated in the future.

Be careful with your conversations about sales. You want assurance that sales will increase to cover the impact of commissions, but galleries may exaggerate sales potential. If they make statements about sales that seem overly optimistic, ask them to put their projections in writing and ask them how many sales can happen in the first sixty days of the relationship. If you expect to have a probationary period in your contract, you can assess their projections as part of your decision of whether or not to remain with the gallery.

Artists, especially young or emerging artists, can be vulnerable when negotiating representation. Some get so emotionally high from the prospect of having a show that they do not ensure that an offer to exhibit (or a representation agreement) is the right one for them. On the other hand, being too careful can put off a gallery. Some artists—again, particularly young or emerging artists—can lose the interest of a gallery by following all the rules outlined in resources such as this one, far too stringently. If the artist comes across as too interested in protecting herself or himself from every conceivable negative outcome with a plethora of contractual clauses with which the gallery director must comply, it may be too much for him or her—especially if the artist does not have a strong history of successes. Just as some directors are difficult for artists, artists can be difficult for directors as well.

Remember, you must objectively assess the gallery as the gallery assesses you and your work. You may even decide to show with one that has a reputation of concern but has, you feel, benefits to offer that outweigh those concerns; you will at least know what to expect from having done your homework. Approach venues that sell work in your price range and, if possible, get an introduction to your targeted gallery representative through artists who know him or her—even better, by artists represented by that gallery.

The Interview

Galleries are generally interested in artists who produce saleable work—work that is appropriate for their roster of best buyers. The gallery sees two routes to sales success: thoroughly professional conduct in an artist with a unique and/or masterful vision and technique, or an artist with extensive previous sales and/or with a large and proven mailing list. And certainly, the artist's personality and productivity are important factors for the gallery director to consider.

If you are seeking representation, some strategists suggest convincing the gallery director that she or he will make money from the sales and licensing of your art. You should appear keen to be an effective partner in generating sales—galleries want a positive sales relationship with the artists they represent. They do not want to work with an artist who spends all his or her time creating art and expecting them to be solely responsible for generating sales. You must prove your marketability and assist in sales. The artist's relationship with a gallery will thrive and endure if there are sales. Sales are the root of the relationship—never forget that.

The artist's relationship with a gallery will thrive and endure if there are sales. Sales are the root of the relationship—never forget that.

Some points to consider when having an interview with a prospective gallery:

1. Make a strong case for the marketability of your art—know why it will be bought (and your reasons should be compatible with the taste of the gallery's clients or the mandate of the gallery). Be able to identify uniqueness in your work and have several points as to how you will produce sales (share information about your mailing list, past buyers, unique advertising opportunities you can access,

and your "personal markets," such as clubs you belong to, alumni organizations, church, etc.).

2. If there are sales hooks in your body of work, share them with the gallery representative. The more marketing ideas you have the better. Otherwise, the gallery may consider less favourable markets for your work when reviewing your portfolio or as a result of seeing past exhibitions if you don't have specific marketing ideas (e.g., if you paint florals, have a list of targeted botanical buyers to offer).
3. Be prepared to offer the names of references—people who have invested in you and love your work, people with whom you have worked, and/or art teachers who have respect and faith in you.
4. If you are an articulate person, and you feel comfortable, or even confident, talking to prospective buyers, offer the gallery those services. (Be careful: not all of you who love to talk have effective communication skills.)
5. Show that you have considerable inventory available when you are seeking representation, and communicate that you have the ability to produce enough inventory to satisfy the gallery over time (but don't make overly enthusiastic and unrealistic promises!).
6. Have (and state) a desire to stick with the gallery for the long term. In seeking a gallery, you are asking someone to invest in you. They need to see a return on that investment which can often only be achieved over time.
7. Mention your capacity to get along well with people and demonstrate this in all your interactions with the gallery and their clients.

Consignment & Representation Agreements

There are two basic types of agreements between an artist and an exhibition/sales outlet: a consignment agreement and a representation agreement.

A consignment agreement covers all responsibilities and all possible eventualities involved with placing your artwork for sale in a sales outlet. Artists using a consignment agreement may have such an agreement with several retail outlets in the same market.

A representation agreement covers the same concerns and it adds a clause or clauses concerned with exclusivity in a defined market area, involves marketing management services, and is designed to be long lasting. A representation agreement with a progressive gallery is a "full service" agreement that includes career management counseling.

Consignment Agreements

Artists consign their work to venues that offer their work for sale without first paying for it. Artists receive payment for consigned work when it is sold—minus the sales commission.

Artists consigning works to a gallery or any other sales outlet must have an agreement in writing that covers all basic concerns. Consultation with your sales outlets and your peers can be very helpful to understand the process and what it entails. Remember, you are in partnership with your outlets—if you sense an adversarial tone, you may be dealing with the wrong retailer. A good agreement will give you effective protection and ensure enduring good relations with your retail outlets.

Not everything presented in the list below of things to consider may be relevant to your consignment agreement, and there may be concerns unique to your market or work that require a customized contract, but the list can be a starting point for you.

Parties: The names and all contact information of the parties to the agreement.

Scope: What inventory level must be maintained? How often will your work be shown or featured? Might there be sales between shows? If so, how will they be generated? Is there a probationary period? Is any exclusivity required?

Duration: The time period of the contract should be defined: Is it to be subject to a certain volume of sales, is it extendable, fixed, renewable? Should there be a probationary period?

Termination: What are the implications to each party to the agreement if a signatory wishes to end the agreement? Can either party terminate the contract? Is notice required?

Administration: Who pays for the framing, crating, and shipping expenses involved with getting your work to the gallery? What are the conditions of storage for consigned work that is not being shown? Can you get easy access to consigned work for reference or to assist with sales?

Insurance: Define who covers work shipped by you to the gallery, by the gallery to a buyer or other sales agent, and to you from the gallery while in the gallery's possession and/or while in the possession of any agent engaged by the gallery.

Damage: Define responsibilities in the event of damage—compensation, treatment, and selection of restoration process and personnel.

Marketing/Sales: Determine exhibition frequency (with times and dates if possible). Define who oversees design of any exhibitions, invitations, ads, and media releases. Know who pays for all marketing and sales costs, including who pays for photographing your work for use in sales and marketing and who owns the copyrights and reproduction rights of the images.

Other marketing/sales points to consider:

- Time payments and the credit risk of time payments.
- The possibility of exchanges or "trade ups" for the buyer. (Such an agreement allows a buyer to return the work in exchange for a new work—usually with a further payment due).
- Return/refund policies, including how long any such policies exist after the date of purchase.
- Any expenses undertaken by the gallery that the gallery expects to be refunded by the artist—how are they authorized?
- Income from lectures, reproduction rights, rentals, et cetera. Which, if any, of these sources of revenue are to be commissioned to the gallery?
- The right to access the name and contact information of all purchasers.

Pricing: Prices should be set in accordance with your price rationale. Your gallery should be a partner in pricing. Discounts should be consultative. Also, you should consider rentals and commissions. (Document all decisions in your inventory diary.)

Payments: Specify when they are to be made; discuss record keeping, access to it and financial reporting.

Representation Agreements

The purpose of a representation agreement is to cover, in writing, every single aspect of the relationship between the artist and the gallery in a way that is agreeable to both parties. A good contractual agreement has each party in possession of a signed and dated copy.

An artist entering this kind of relationship agrees that the gallery has exclusive rights to the sale of the artist's work and services in a defined market area (usually the city in which the exhibition/sales outlet functions—often an even wider market). A representation agreement can be negotiated to any mutually satisfying terms between the artist and the gallery—but there is usually a concern for exclusivity. In such an agreement, the gallery earns a percentage of all sales *except* on sales exempted by mutual arrangement.

Galleries, dealers, consultants, curators, and publishers often have existing agreements or contracts. You should read them carefully and consider consulting peer professionals, a lawyer, or a trusted artist-friend before signing one. You should strive to understand everything in the contract. If you have any questions about a clause, or if you feel a clause, as read, does not properly express its intent, ask the gallery to explain it for you in writing and append the interpretation to the agreement copies of both parties bearing the signed initials of the gallery director.

It is also a good idea to invest some time to create your own contract—put together one that gives you confidence, building on an existing model. Sample agreements are available through various sources, including: galleries, dealers, or fellow artists; professional development books and websites for visual artists; and visual art service organizations or clubs in your area. (*See Appendix B for sample contract clauses.*)

Artists are advised, however, not to copy a standard agreement or contract, no matter how good it appears to be. All such sources should be viewed as advisory. They can provide guidance on language, structure, and content, but due diligence is the key. A modest investment of research, writing, and legal consultation can provide artists with a contract for a lifetime. Perhaps the best source of contractual advice for visual artists (plus sample contracts) is CARFAC Ontario's publication, *Artists' Contracts*. (*See chapter thirteen to learn more about CARFAC, Canada's national association for visual artists.*)

A Note About Insurance

When you place work for sale in a venue, it is tempting to use the gallery's insurance if they offer it to you while your work is in their possession. However, if an unfortunate circumstance arises that requires you to make an insurance claim, you may find yourself unable to contact the gallery's insurer (if there ever was one) or that the policy is out of date or premiums were not paid. Therefore, although it can mean extra administrative responsibility, it is wise to consider insuring your work yourself when placing it in a sales venue.

Discounts

Galleries often have favoured clients. They may be key curators or collectors or a corporation with an extensive purchase history. These clients may be offered discounts by your gallery—often 10% to 20%. This practice should be discussed as part of your representation or consignment agreement; you should approve all discounts in advance of them being offered. Galleries often expect the discount to be shared by the artist, leaving you with less income than you expect from some sales.

Conflict Resolution

Even with an agreement in place, things can go wrong. When they do, it is often due to the lack of business ethics on the part of one of the contractual parties. Artists can disappoint galleries by creating work that is not up to par, unframed, arrives late, or is damaged and/or unfinished. Or, they may provide simplistic artist statements, be unwilling to assist the gallery with media interviews or sales, or make sales in the gallery's market area without informing or commissioning the gallery. Artists must, in every way and to the best of their ability, live up to all terms of an agreement with their galleries.

Of greater concern is the disreputable gallery operator. Galleries will often not provide buyers names and contact information; this is fair practice if they are providing you with dynamic representation but not fair if their marketing on your behalf is less than aggressive and ongoing. Some galleries take too long to pay for work sold; some discount work without first obtaining the artist's permission to do so, and some may damage, lose or steal artwork. The disreputable gallery owner who disappears in the night or claims no responsibility for "lost" or "stolen" items deserves to be reported to the police. Reporting those who break the law helps other artists from suffering the same fate. If you find yourself in the unfortunate position of discovering your gallery is disreputable, there is comfort and advice available to Canadian artists through the website, "Gallery Owe: artists united against unscrupulous dealers; des artistes unis contre les galeristes malhonnêtes" (*galleryowe.blogspot.com*).

If you are ever to consult with a lawyer, the best time to do it is before you sign a contract and not when you have a problem. This is not an essential step for most artists, but a lawyer's advice is best used as a preventive service. Also, if your work sells at high prices, you might be well advised to have your contract reviewed by a lawyer. An attorney can offer valuable feedback on any proposed contractual partnership, explaining the implications or meanings of contract clauses, highlighting potential conflicts or areas that are vulnerable to interpretation, and/or suggesting overlooked clauses. Attorneys specialize, so artists considering legal action should consult legal referral services or non-profit arts legal services in their area, or inquire with another gallery or colleagues, to find the appropriate legal office that specializes in contractual law and that has knowledge of the visual art world and visual art marketing practices.

When problems do emerge, do all that is possible to resolve the differences between you and your gallery. Take time between discussions and set guidelines; agree to be respectful and to try to avoid emotional language. If discussion proves fruitless, identify resolution resources and governing laws in your area. If the problem is financial, it may be resolved by means of a payment plan. If discussion cannot resolve the issue, the artist can also consider small claims court for resolution of a financial problem. Going to small claims court will often bring you financial compensation for provable loss, damage, or theft of artwork. Going to court should only be considered when (and if) the artist has lots of documentation for all claims—especially on the value of the artwork(s) in question.

If neither discussion nor small claims court can resolve a problem, the next step to consider, in effort to avoid the time and expense of court action, is mediation. Mediation can be proposed constructively whereas legal action is always confrontational. Mediation is a remarkably effective service for people involved in a conflict that engages the emotions of the parties involved. The mediator brings skills to the discussion that allow the parties to focus exclusively on the issue, and mediation is far less expensive than court action—you share the cost of the mediator with your adversary. (You can also consult a lawyer to privately guide you in the mediation process if need be.)

In the end, however, sometimes the best advice is that if you feel that you must take your gallery to court—don't! Only consider it if there is a huge financial loss and/or if you are wealthy. No matter how you see things or no matter how badly you feel, the court system is not a place for artists. With luck, the lawyer you approach will help you see the futility of seeking redress in the courts. The lawyer may have alternative suggestions to court, if he or she is a good lawyer. It is often best in the long run, and for your wallet, to "let go" of your issue and to "move on"—most issues between a gallery and an artist are not life threatening, and often, the artist with ego and pride issues can overreact. It is important to keep things in perspective.

FOUR

Submitting to Curators & Juries

"Listen carefully to first criticisms made of your work. Note just what it is about your work that critics don't like—then cultivate it. That's the only part of your work that's individual and worth keeping."

—*Jean Cocteau*

"I was once responsible for 600 artists getting equal and fair treatment from a jury. We had to provide the jurors with a book containing 600 artist statements in a certain order, and a second book containing the artists' résumés in the same order. As well, we had to organize the 3,000 slides into carousels—all in the same order. And then, when the jurying was finished, we had to reassemble all the discordant pieces in order to return all the submissions. I learned a thing or two from that experience!"— *C. T.*

Introduction

This chapter is concerned with the selection process of non-profit art galleries, artist cooperatives, and public "calls for entry" where there is often less-to-no concern with sales. This should only be the concern of career artists with considerable experience who are able to knowledgeably articulate their aesthetic philosophy.

Non-profit galleries are usually government-funded, provincially registered societies operating as federally registered charities. In urban settings, these galleries serve artists seeking critical reviews of their work and the advancement of their careers. Usually, curators or curatorial committees are the primary contacts of the artists seeking exhibitions in publicly funded institutions.

Another type of gatekeeper—functioning between the artist and gallery—is the visual art jury. A jury is a group of individuals functioning as the curator of a space, competition, or exhibition. Many artists will already be familiar with these gatekeepers of public (non-profit) visual art spaces and events, but it is important to be clear about their roles and duties.

Who Is a Curator?

Curators are stewards of collections. They are the primary caretakers of the objects in the collections of archives, libraries, galleries, museums, individual and corporate collections, and botanical gardens.

The curator's role may include some or all of these tasks:

1. Collecting objects.
2. Making provisions for the effective preservation, conservation, interpretation, documentation, research, and display of a collection.
3. Making the collection accessible to the public.

Most visual artists and the general public become aware of curators in their capacity of organizer of exhibitions—a curator (or a director acting as a curator) runs most public (non-profit) galleries. In the past, curators often had degrees in fine art; today, many curators have degrees in curatorial studies. Curators are either employees of visual art organizations and are attached to a specific institution, or they freelance, proposing projects to the resident curators of institutions.

Curators can also be thought of as tellers of stories. They tell and interpret stories with both imagery (the artifacts themselves) and any accompanying text. The exhibitions or stories are revelatory: by seeing a large number of pieces by one artist or by viewing the images of several artists in one exhibition, viewers find deeper meanings through the relationships between the images, and by doing so they discover the thread of the curator's intension in creating the exhibition. The curator's story is told in the artifacts themselves, as well as in the catalogues, artist statements, narrative of gallery docents, and sometimes in text panels that are part of the exhibition.

As stewards of our heritage, curators working in public institutions have a responsibility to tell us the most interesting or most important stories of, and for, their constituencies. They are responsible to the local taxpayers (the general public whose taxes support the institution), the artists of their community, and the members, sponsors, and donors of their organizations. They must show us the best of our local, provincial, and national artists—those artists who excel at interpreting who we are and those who make a significant contribution to contemporary art practice. And, when possible, curators should show us the work of very significant artists from outside our communities. The role of the curator in a public institution, or the institution's curatorial objective, is often defined in the institution's constitution or mandate.

Curators also function significantly in the lives of Canadian visual artists because of the role they often play in the peer jurying process of the Canada Council for the Arts and other funding agencies. Their regional knowledge of artists helps coordinate public investment in individual artists and/or art practices. Artists who are often featured in the exhibitions of significant public institutions are those who become part of our cultural heritage. Art critics, dealers, and collectors pay particular attention to the artists who capture the interest of curators.

Curators are also responsible for knowing what is going on in their communities—provincially, nationally, and internationally. The specific responsibilities vary from institution to institution; some curators focus on the art from a defined geographical region whereas others may specialize in a medium or genre of art. Curating is a creative and intellectual activity designed to provoke thought about a thesis. It is a process of narration, assembling the work of artists around a theme, issue, or concern. The curatorial process can address the relevance and interconnections between the works of diverse artists or it can focus on the work of a single artist that revealing new insights into his or her process.

Curators who work in an institutional environment (the large public galleries) have to shape the thesis of their exhibitions in the context of their gallery's mandate, its academic/aesthetic worth, and its relation to the institutional audience. Their exhibitions often have to serve as a basis for public-funding applications, so they must be meritorious. Curators approach artists, galleries, and collectors for work to include in their exhibitions—for work that supports their thesis.

A curator can become aware of you by reading a review of your work in the media, seeing your work in an exhibition, hearing a word-of-mouth reference from other visual artists, or by your own efforts to meet her or him in person. Many contemporary artists have representation by a commercial gallery and seek to exhibit in public galleries as well. Their shows in commercial galleries can serve as a means of introduction to curators (and vice versa). No matter how it comes to be that an artist has an interview or studio visit with a curator, the artist should be properly prepared.

The "Professional" Artist

For the purposes of this chapter, a specific meaning of the word "professional" is worth considering, as is an understanding that the curators of "flagship" institutions in our urban centres have an elite curatorial role. Artists should understand that these galleries serve the "professional artist" who, as defined by the Canada Council for the Arts, is someone who:

1. Has specialized training in the field (not necessarily in academic institutions).
2. Is recognized as such by his or her peers.
3. Is committed to devoting more time to artistic activity, if financially feasible.
4. Has produced an independent body of work.
5. Has made at least three public presentations of work in a professional context over a three-year period.

6. Has maintained an independent professional practice for at least three years. (Students are not eligible.)

Support Materials

Before you approach a non-profit gallery or public institution about an exhibition or about purchasing your work for a public collection, you should have all the appropriate support materials that you will need in place. This includes business cards, résumé, artist statement, slides (properly labeled), a website, your portfolio. All the support materials should advance your case for including your work at that venue, but there should be nothing superfluous, redundant, or repetitive in your message; whatever and all that you present should be integrated, create impact, and provide exactly the right amount of information that they will need. Also, the language that you use in all your self-promotion materials must be appropriate *(see the Language Choices section of chapter eight and see chapter eleven.)*

Tips on Approaching Curators or Non-Profit Galleries

Only approach curators/galleries relevant to your work. Be clear about your intentions: Are you wanting a show? Do you want the gallery to buy your work for their collection? Aim to be seen by the curators of galleries where artists you admire show their work.

Visit the gallery in which you want an exhibition. Go often and regularly, and let staff get to know you if possible. Visit the gallery's website and read all that relates to its mandate, procedures, and policies. Talk to artists who have shown at the gallery to learn more about the space, its staff, and policies.

Identify the appropriate contact (the curator, program director, or executive director) for your submission. If the gallery's application and/or selection procedures for slide review are not posted on its website or otherwise available to you, contact the curator by email or phone for advice.

Do not assume that you can submit your images to a curator via email. Many curators and galleries prefer that images be provided on a CD or DVD or as slides. The best colour representation by far is achieved through slides.

Be patient. Give curators and galleries time to respond; they receive many submissions. If you have talked to the person to whom you have submitted material, wait a month before contacting her or him again if you have not received a response. If you have submitted to a curator or gallery "on spec" and with no invitation to submit, wait longer.

Always include an SASE (self-addressed stamped envelope) with each submission. This increases the likelihood of them returning your slides and materials. Some artists also include a stamped self-addressed postcard that allows the gallery to acknowledge that they have received their submission.

Do not repeat your artist statement when discussing your art with a curator in person. Be prepared to deal passionately with the ideas behind your work, your inspirations, your references, and objectives.

Highlight your media exposure and/or critical reviews. Achieve as much media exposure and critical reviews as possible from your work in commercial galleries, artist-run spaces, and/or exhibitions of your own creation. Publicity opens many doors, but is not always easy to obtain. Media exposure and reviews will not get you in a curator's door, but if your work is exceptional in some way, the publicity may help "open the door" to curatorial interest.

Arrange for exhibitions of your work in other cities/countries (if you can), this will add credence to your career and résumé.

Work on your listening and speaking skills. If you get an interview, focus as much on your listening skills as you do on speaking skills when making a presentation. Do not digress and make sure your self-editor is on alert when speaking with a curator. Stay focused, do not speak for too long, and try to be relaxed.

Remember it is a totally subjective process; be prepared for rejection and handle it professionally (*see chapter fourteen*).

Cold Calling

The sales term, "cold calling," describes the process of approaching prospective clients (usually by phone) who have no expectation of your call. It describes any situation where one person calls someone without an established prior relationship. Artists who send submissions to curators with whom they have never spoken are cold calling them. The following comments about cold calling were solicited from curators who were promised anonymity.

Curator A: "In summary, I want to emphasize that artists must do their research. They should know about my specialty and our gallery's mandate, and they should be familiar with our exhibition history before they approach me. Calling or writing to me should be the culminating act of a strategy that has the applicant learning about us over a decent length of time. Applicants should understand our process, attend our programs, such as our artist talks (these events are far more important than our openings), and meet and get to know some of the artists who have a strong relationship with us and who have exhibited in our gallery."

Curator B: "Hundreds of artists send us submissions every year. We eventually get to see each one and we ask those artists whose work interests us if we can keep their materials on file for reference. Although we would not likely offer an artist an exhibition opportunity based on a submission, we do provide our reference material as a resource for guest curators, visiting curators, and scholars. We offer exhibitions to artists with whom we have a relationship over time. Local artists are best served by our gallery through our assessment sessions that provide artists with time with our curators for a portfolio review and commentary. These sessions are very practical for both the artists and the gallery."

Curator C: "Most artists I meet would be better off directing the time, thought, energy, and talent they put into meeting curators into self-promotional activities that further their exposure and career. Let us discover you doing what you do best—making art that attracts the visually curious."

Curator D: "Cold calling, as you call it, can work in our community because we are a regional gallery serving a large part of the province. I welcome it as long as adequate postage is provided on an SASE. I try to keep up with submissions, but I can get up to fifteen to twenty a week. The best thing artists can do is to not call me; I'll get there. Remember—your submission was unsolicited. If your work is striking in some way, I will arrange for a studio visit but that does not mean a showing of your work will ensue. You may come to mind for an exhibition—of mine or a colleague's—or you may not."

Curator E: "I respect that artists' need to solicit my attention and that of other curators, but I almost exclusively use artists whom I have known for a long time. If you send something to me and don't hear from me, it means I see no reason for us to meet. And that is not a comment on the worthiness of your work per se. It is a comment on the relevance of your work to me and my institution's aesthetic mission."

Artist-Run Spaces

Artist-run spaces are visual art hotspots. These exhibition spaces are often operated as non-profit societies and have boards of directors and a defined curatorial process. They are excellent venues for artists to show new work; they are often spaces that curators of other galleries watch for new talent. Artist-run spaces also offer exhibitors a community of peers that can serve many purposes. As with galleries, there is usually a right artist-run space to approach depending on the nature of your work. Do your homework and research all such spaces, choosing the right one(s) for you. Follow the same guidelines as you would for a meeting with a curator in approaching these spaces.

Exhibiting with an artist-run centre or artist collective is good practice for artists wishing to base their careers on showing in public galleries and getting critical reviews. Besides these centres, however, exhibition and peer access can also be available to artists through sketch clubs, discipline cooperatives (such as printmakers and sculptors, who need space and share expensive equipment), artists' guilds, and/or local arts councils—there are numerous forms of visual arts (or general arts) collectives that provide artists with opportunities. Just a little research on the web or through community resources, such as local college art departments, government arts offices, libraries, and arts councils, may help artists find a venue. The application/selection process for the exhibition programs of guilds, clubs, or artist-run centres is usually available on their websites or by means of a telephone call.

Getting involved with a visual art collective can rapidly expand your network. Building a network of connections means becoming part of your local community of artists, and these connections can be an instrumental part of the process of getting noticed by a curator. Many artists meet curators by means of a personal reference from another artist. The visual art world is a small one. Getting to know others (and getting known yourself) can be quite easy for a determined, clever, and talented artist—especially one with confidence. If you immerse yourself in the local art scene and go to lots of events, you will be able to identify the key individuals with whom to network, such as other artists, gallery owners, critics, collectors, writers, and curators. And get involved—become a volunteer or a member of a visual art organization where you fit best. (And, get all your contacts onto a mailing list [*see chapter six*].)

Submitting to Juried Shows

In a juried exhibition, a panel of individuals replaces the curator. A visual art jury is a small group of professional artists who are charged with selecting work for an exhibition—work that is usually submitted by a call for entry. While curators are charged with researching artists to include in their shows—work that supports the aesthetic thesis of their exhibition—juries make their selections for exhibitions from works submitted to their call for entry. The story, theme, purpose, or objective of juried shows is outlined in the call. Artists responding to a call are usually asked to provide biographical information, five slides or more of their work, an artist statement about the work, an entry fee, and an SASE in which to return your materials.

Juried shows can have any number of purposes or objectives: artistic, educational, or practical. They sometimes serve as fundraisers for the host organization when entrance fees and sales commissions are charged. (Curators and academics sometimes view juried exhibitions as having limited artistic integrity.)

Open & Blind Juries

In an open jury, jurists view the submitting artists' slides along with their biographical information and artist statements. The open jury, therefore, considers more than just the work. Jury members know the name of the applicants and can assess each applicant's level of career development from the résumé provided.

In a blind jury, jurists only view the slides of all the applicants to the exhibition. A blind jury does not know who the artists are when they are viewing the slides (unless they recognize the work, technique, or subject of a submitted work). They are provided with neither the artists' résumés nor their statements. Blind juries are an attempt on the part of exhibition organizers to minimize prejudice and focus their selections on the work and not on the artists' careers.

Responding to Calls for Entry

Sometimes artists can respond to a call for entry with work that they already have produced; sometimes they may want to create new work that responds to the call. Sometimes calls require that the submitted work has never been shown before, or that it be completed within a recent and defined period of time. If a call does not include jurying, be wary of being part of such an exhibition. Such a show is fine for the amateur artist not interested in sales or career development, but it is not relevant, in most cases, to the committed and serious artist seeking professional status.

A call for entry from a gallery can be an ideal opportunity to present yourself if you are beginning your career or live in a small city. Submitting to a call is good practice for an artist if it is from a reputable gallery, artist collective, or jury. If the gallery issuing the call has been around for a long time, or if the call relates to a recurring annual exhibition with a strong history, submitting to such a call can be worth the time of an emerging artist. When an annual or biannual juried show has a long history—over ten years—be aware that there will be more competition and a lower acceptance rate. Artists have to have to present a strong submission if they want to gain entry into established juried shows. Provincial, national, and/or international juried exhibitions are highly competitive; artists submitting to ones of this scale should have some local, juried show experience before applying.

Tips on Responding to Juried Calls

Follow call-for-entry instructions carefully, and if you are not clear on what to do or how to do what is requested, contact the organizers so that you understand the submission requirements completely. Five slides means five slides, not more. When artist statements are limited to one page, be sure to do that. If submissions must be mailed through Canada Post, do not send emails.

Submit slides of your work rather than print materials, such as photographs or photocopies. Print materials are hard to circulate to jurists and they are often not as clear, sharp, and colour-accurate as slides can be. Label slides clearly, uniformly, and completely; follow established traditions in slide labeling (*see Appendix C, Slide Notes Sheet*).

Follow formatting, resolution/density, and size directions carefully, if digital images are to be submitted (*see Appendix D, Digital Images Note Sheet*).

Type. Handwritten submissions can often be misinterpreted.

Be clear, precise, concise, and error-free in your written submissions.

Pay attention to scale limitations. If your work is absolutely huge or extremely heavy, practical considerations on the part of organizers may have you eliminated easily. If you are submitting something physically or technologically challenging, call organizers before you submit. Provide organizers with the reassurance they need to keep physically challenging work eligible during the jurying. (Offer to do all the moving, prearrange delivery, and/or to provide any necessary equipment, for example.)

A Note on Rejection

Receiving no call back, or a "thanks, but no thanks" message? Don't worry. Consider it a skin-thickening experience. Your submission was not a wasted effort, but taking the rejection personally is a waste of energy and time. Just shrug your shoulders and carry on (*see chapter fourteen for more on rejection*).

FIVE

Donating to Charity Visual Art Auctions

"An artist cannot fail; it is a success to be one."

—*Charles Horton Cooley*

"I hope that those artists who can afford to donate art for a charity auction make a priority of helping non-profit visual art organizations."

—*C. T.*

Artists Empathize

Artists are often highly emotional individuals. Their compassion can be easily exploited by charitable organizations that undertake auctions as fundraisers. Moved by the social objectives of the auction organizers, artists often say yes to requests to donate art for an auction without thinking about the cost. Given the low income of most artists, it seems unfair to expect them to support social causes when our society does so little to support artists.

Artists are the face of many social causes—they care about the environment, education, health, and culture; they care about justice and fairness, and their souls naturally want to support those causes in which they believe. We can be rightfully proud of all that society derives from the international community of artists, but we have to be practical.

Issues around art auctions and donations by artists are a concern of CARFAC (Canadian Artists' Representation/Le Front des artistes canadiens) a national, visual art and professional artists' advocacy organization (*see chapter thirteen*). Their national office published a 1994 advisory note "Guidelines for Professional Standards in the Organization of Fund-Raising Events" and an article in their 2006 fall/winter newsletter on the subject. Visit the CARFAC website, carfac.ca, to access the newsletter.

Some Statistics

The financial reporting of five Vancouver visual art organizations reveals how much money was raised by their charity auctions during a six-week period in the fall of 1999: the Federation of Canadian Artists' AIM for the Arts event had sales of $66,400; the Contemporary Art Gallery auction sold $65, 275 worth of art; the Vancouver Art Gallery live auction took in $350,000 in sales and its silent auction took in $63,775; and the art auctions for the Vancouver Friends for Life Society and the Arts Umbrella earned $88,900 and $164,150, respectively. It is amazing that there was $734,725 worth of local art sold through these events in so short a time. Clearly, the charity auction is a major medium for the sale of contemporary visual art.

Some art auctions expect that the artists donate their work. The obvious problem with this model of partnership is that the artists receive no income for the sale of their work. Another problem for the artists is receipting. Tax receipts may be not forthcoming in a timely fashion, for a value that the artists did not accept, or not tax deductible because the issuing society was not a federally registered charity or was non-compliant with federal and/or provincial filing responsibilities.

Provincially registered non-profit society status does not qualify the organization to issue tax-deductible receipts; only a federally registered charity in full compliance can do that legally. Before donating to any auction, be sure to determine that the sanctioning body is a federally registered charity in compliance with all reporting requirements.

Some fundraising art auctions are staged by charities that share sales revenues with the contributing artists. Often, minimum prices are agreed on prior to the event. This is an important development that makes the process far fairer for the artist—especially when you consider the following:

1. At the Arts Umbrella auction, art by forty-nine artists valued at $203,575 (set by the artists) sold for a total of $164,150.

2. At the Vancouver Friends for Life Society's Art for Life auction, art by thirty-one artists valued at $108,350 sold for $88,900.

3. At the Vancouver Art Gallery live auction, forty-six artists offered work valued at $325,950, and at the silent auction, thirty artists offered work valued at $63,775. Together, the two VAG auctions put $389,725 worth of art on sale, and auction revenue was close to an even $350,000.

In the Arts Umbrella auction, the contributing artists collectively lost a total of $39,425 worth of potential sales. At the Art for Life auction, artists

Example: Sophia

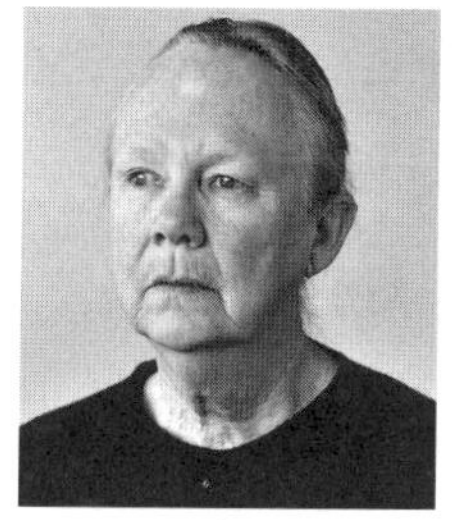

Sophia is both an artist and a collector. "I would advise all artists to never donate artwork to medical or hospital group, school, or police or firefighter auctions," she says. "At least the big gallery/museum/art school auctions attract the right audiences who respect art and artists, and the prices generally go above reserves. I was at a non-art related silent auction recently where the highest bid on a painting was $20. I was so offended that someone would be so disrespectful that I placed the next bid at $250 and took the work home."

lost a total of $19,450. The two Vancouver Art Gallery auctions created $39,725 worth of lost potential revenue. During the six-week period in 1999, artists lost a total of $98,600!

On the other hand, during those six months and through only five events, local contemporary visual artists sold a total of $734,725 worth of art. That is quite a figure. And all of it (except the money raised for Art for Life) was raised to support valued local visual art organizations.

Terms

The conditions of sale for your donation are up to you to negotiate. One important thing to consider is the value of the receipt. Sometimes, the auction organizers will want to issue you a receipt for the value of the final sale price of the piece. When this is well below the price-per-square-inch value you set for the piece, you should challenge the agency and get a replacement receipt, using your inventory diary to substantiate its value. Your receipt should be for the value of your donation and not for the value of the auction sale price.

Several visual art service organizations advise their members to say no to donating art. Saying yes further encourages the practice of exploiting some of our nation's poorest professionals to subsidize social growth. But, if and when a cause close to your heart makes it impossible to say no, at least take steps to ensure that you also benefit from the experience by being treated well and promptly receipted. Do not support exploitative auctions.

If you are considering donating your artwork, ask questions. Find out who are the organizers and the background of the charity. Ask about past auctions: How many people attended? What is the demographic? What is the sales history? How many auctions have the organizers done in the past? Ask for referrals—have them arrange for an artist in one of their previous auctions to contact you to interview him or her about the charity's professionalism.

The Association of Fundraising Professionals advises members undertaking charity art auctions to have a prospectus for contributing artists. The prospectus should include: standards for pricing and receipting, evaluation policy (for the issuing of tax receipts), names of jurors, deadlines, framing responsibilities, and payment method and date.

If you are considering donating a work of art to an art auction organizer, be sure to:

1. Ask for a prospectus or equivalent documentation.
2. Offer to sell the work to the charity at your wholesale price instead.
3. Expect a receipt in line with your price rationale if you donate your work.
4. Contractually agree to a reserve bid (your price-per-square-inch wholesale price) and get your work back if it is not met.
5. Contractually agree for the contact information of the buyer of your work (to send the buyer a thank-you note, biographical information, and inform him or her of your future exhibitions and sales).
6. Expect documentation on the sale price of your work.
7. Identify who is insuring your work as it is in transit and during the auction.
8. Be extremely wary of charities operating online auctions—always decline these requests, unless you do a lot of homework into the legitimacy of the auction and its sponsoring agency.

Attending the Auction

William is a successful First Nations artist. He is a very savvy professional artist—he makes his choices carefully as to which charities to support with donations of his art. When he receives a request, he follows many of the steps outlined above, and at the conclusion of all the negotiations, he asks one simple question: "Will you be sending me two tickets to the event or am I to pick them up at the door?" If organizers are not prepared to host him at the event when he is donating a piece of art worth well over $1,000, he withdraws from the auction. "It's about respect," he says, "but it is also good business." He fervently believes that his presence at the event boosts the sale price of his work, and by attending, he meets many people to add to his mailing list.

Charity auctions are often gala dinners with buyers seated at tables. William noticed that at two auctions one year, the buyers of his works were sitting at his table. They had formed a relationship with him during dinner and wanted to own a piece of his work. Consequently, he sees his attendance at the galas as valuable both for him and for the auction organizers.

Charities that have a policy of hosting donating artists earn the ongoing support of artists, according to William, and higher auction sales.

Tips for Artist-Donators

The best art auctions to support are those that support the visual arts and visual artists. Their events attract the right audience for artists involved with career advancement. Donate to non-visual art auctions only when you believe strongly in the cause. Such auctions will likely not advance your career.

Donate a work appropriate to the taste of the attendees. Ask organizers for assistance in choosing the right work in aesthetic terms. Also ask them about average sale prices of pieces—choose a piece that is worth an average auction bid.

Choose to donate a good work, not the one that never sells. The work you donate represents you and your career to all attendees.

Have promotional material for the buyer: encourage auction organizers to provide your buyer with your résumé or other biographical information.

Be "creative" with how you donate. Another model of donation that artists can often successfully negotiate entails the charity purchasing the artwork for the full retail value and the artist then sending a cheque to the charity for 50% of the value of the work. The artist gets a tax-deductible receipt for the donation as well as her or his wholesale price, and the charity sets the minimum bid at 50% of the purchase price. This model is a winning one for all involved.

Do not agree to pay for the appraisal. The Canada Revenue Agency requires that an independent expert must appraise the donor's artwork to determine the fair market value. Some charities insist on having one or even two such appraisals before they will issue a receipt, and they often require the appraisal to be paid for by the artist. Rather than paying for an appraisal, artists should offer letters from their galleries, inventory diary records, or contact information of past buyers to prove the work's value.

Comments by a Tax Expert

Robert McMurray, artist, accountant, and author of the chapter on taxation in this primer (*see chapter twelve*) writes: "I would suggest to some charities that they are being overly zealous about getting appraisals. If they cannot provide an official receipt based on my written assurance that the amount is my standard gallery price established by past transactions and that the same amount will be reported as deemed income in my tax return, then I am not likely to bless them with one of my masterpieces.

"Artists have an option that is not available to most other taxpayers in that they can set the value of their work anywhere between zero and fair market value. The greatest benefit of this option is derived if the artist is in the lower of four tax brackets. The benefit decreases as the bracket increases.

"Lets look at an example: Sharon is a single artist living in BC and she has part-time income of $28,000. She derives no profit from the sale of her work (she breaks even) and she is considering donating a painting with an assessed value of $2,000. Without the donation, Sharon's taxable income $28,000 and her income tax due is $4,204.

"If she declares the income from the donation, her taxable income is $30,000 *but* she also earns a valuable tax credit. The addition income of $2,000 is taxed at the low rate of 21%, increasing her taxes by $420, but the donation credit on $2,000 is calculated at the high rate of 41.5%, decreasing her taxes due by $830. The result is a net tax decrease of $410—her income tax payable becomes only $3,794."

SIX

Marketing Your Art

"Making money is art and working is art and good business is the best art." —*Andy Warhol*

"Here is the crux of the issue for many artists: balancing one's artistic integrity with the need to make market-appropriate product." —*C. T.*

Introduction

Beginning with an image of the cave drawings in Lascaux, France, let your imagination take you on a walk through the images you have seen and admired in the museums you have visited throughout your lifetime. Think of the collections of the Uffizi, Hermitage, Louvre, Pitti Palace, and Britain's National Gallery. Most of the artwork that you see in your imaginary tour was created as a visual record for a largely illiterate society. What we also see in the historical pieces is work that a member of the secular and clerical aristocracy commissioned—made to specific order for the commissioner, and often to glorify the commissioner (or a saint or god). Many of those pieces are made to create a vision for the public eye of a social, political, or religious leader posing at a critical moment of his or her career. This business model of working to commission was how many of the greatest painters paid their bills.

The best example of the "paint to please" artist is he who painted the commissioner's portrait from a "mirror" image, figuratively speaking. By painting his client's mirror image, he created a portrait that matched his client's self-perception (as opposed how the artist and everyone else saw the portrait's subject). He did this to ensure that his subject liked what he saw. He also did this to ensure that there would be more commissions from his client and the client's friends.

Few contemporary artists work to commission. Contemporary artists who do work to commission as our great artists once did—architects, graphic designers, and many photographers, for example—are considered "commercial" artists today. Many artists who self-identify as a "professional" are those who create work for themselves, without the parameters of an outside party such as a commissioner; they have an inner drive to create and their concern for the marketplace is anywhere from none-at-all to completely.

And here is the crux of the issue for many artists: balancing their responsibility to the muse (one's artistic integrity) with their need to make an income through the sale of their creations. The ideal marketplace for artists is one that embraces the work of artists of integrity who are strictly and exclusively focused on their work in blissful disregard of commerce. But this happens to very few artists, even to the extent that they can support themselves and their families from their work. Far more artists who do derive a healthy income from their creative practice create their work with the marketplace in mind—in varying degrees. Sometimes the marketplace finds you; sometimes you have to create your market. Although many artists have a desire to earn some percentage of their living from the execution of their creative work, a surprising number are naïve about operating effectively as a small business—and it is, after all, what artists are: small business manufacturers.

The Positive Mindset

In the hierarchy of contemporary visual art culture, the artists who are held in the highest regard are those who create without regard for the marketplace, showing their work in public galleries, and receiving frequent and positive reviews. Conversely, artists at the other end of the continuum, who create art exclusively for the marketplace, can be viewed as having "sold out" as commercial artists. The culture's preference is that the market finds the artist; the artist who seeks success in the marketplace often lives with a sense of being "second class." But if you want to earn a living (or part of your living) from making art, you must embrace—or at least respect—the marketplace. There can always be an argument for those concerned with "selling out": there are many artists who successfully sell work without the market compromising their creative voice.

The artist who creates non-commissioned art and who hopes to make a living—or part of a living—from the sales of her or his art is choosing to operate as a small business. She or he is becoming a manufacturer—not a mass producer (that is the antithesis of artistry), but a small business producing unique pieces as singles or as multiples. She or he invests time, talent, and materials in the creation of art intended for sale; he or she is investing in inventory that is often unproven and not market tested in merchandizing terms.

Many artists make this decision without much of an understanding about the business implications—implications that can have a drastic effect on the odds of success. Operating a small business with a goal of having it sustain the artist (and perhaps the artist's family) is taking on an enormous challenge. When you undertake to seriously grow a small artistic business, you must become a multi-tasker, with a PhD in time management. You must divide your time into units for creation, administration, and marketing—all in an appropriate ratio. Understanding yourself as a small business and operating with sound business strategies will multiply your potential for success.

What Is Marketing?

Marketing is a business-growth activity. It is an all-encompassing philosophy that informs all your decision-making as a small business operator/artist. Good marketers centre their business on the fulfillment of their customers' needs. The best-known components of the marketing mix of activities—pricing, advertising, and promotion/publicity—are made with the customer in mind. Effective marketing means knowing what are people's needs, wants, and demands in regards to the marketplace:

1. Needs drive sales in the purchasing of products and/or services in the marketplace. Our needs are many: there are the physical needs, such as food and protective clothing, and there are the social needs of shelter, a secure environment, and a community and feeling of belonging; and there are the emotional and spiritual needs of feeling loved and self-fulfilled that include the needs for recognition and reward. These are all basic human needs and part of what it is to be human.
2. Wants can be described as those things that satisfy our needs, and our wants can be attainable or not.
3. Demands are the products we actually use to satisfy our needs. The "demands" are our affordable "wants."

For example, Mary buys a new home that is much larger than her previous home and she has much more wall space in her new apartment. She decides that she *needs* art for her walls that is stunningly beautiful and captures the attention and passion of all who enter her new home. What Mary *wants* is art that says to her visitors that this woman is sophisticated and has good taste. She *wants* art that makes her living space more interesting and more beautiful. What she *wants* is Picassos, Cezannes, and Monets. But what she *demands* is local work that she can afford.

If you think about how to fill the demands of your customers, you are doing effective marketing. You will communicate to the marketplace effectively by "selling" your products and services to the right customer and in the right language. Whether you are offering an artistic product or service, you will maximize your potential for success by communicating with your customers in a way that recognizes their needs, wants, and demands. Customers must make choices in fulfilling their needs. Your marketing involves helping the right group of customers make the choice of your products or services over other similar products and services that are available.

Making Your Marketing Plan

By thinking of yourself as a business, you help to remove the ego in the decision-making process. As a self-employed manufacturer, you may have trouble separating yourself and your work, but by thinking of yourself as small business, you can help objectify business decisions—sometimes it is better to ask yourself, "What is the right business decision?" instead of, "What am I going to do?"

Is marketing easy? No. It is hard work. It keeps you out of the studio and is only part of the businessperson's growth strategy. You must increase inventory production as well as time for communications when you implement a marketing plan, because marketing produces growth. It is not every artist's choice, to be businesslike, but for those who want success in the marketplace, a good marketing strategy is very important.

The Mission Statement

Just as a life's purpose is the development of an identity, so must your artistic life have a clear sense of purpose—a mission—that is the base of your business strategy. Most artists need only a simple declarative statement of purpose. Mission statements should be concise, specific, and measurable; they should explain what you do, for whom, and why you exist (how you are unique in the marketplace). Here are two examples:

1. A mission statement that is too vague: "Marble Designs seeks to create the best hand-made paper cards and stationery available in our market and to sell our products at affordable (reasonable; the lowest) prices."
2. A better mission statement: "Marble Designs intends to be the

'source of choice' for customers seeking high-quality, varied, and unique personal correspondence products in Vancouver and in particular, Kitsilano."

To help you frame a statement, consider what it is you do. Are you an artist using a single medium? Are you an artist producing a wide variety of products at different price points? Do you offer services? Is your studio rentable for a day or for longer periods? Do you teach? Are you available for consultations? Is your artistic business full- or part-time?

What is the size and location of your market? Is your only market in your hometown, or is it worldwide (it could be considered so if you sell your work online)?

The larger and/or more diverse your practice, the more important there be a clear statement of intent. Sometimes missions must be reviewed or rewritten after a period of time; they help you, your customers (and your employees if you have any) remember exactly what your business is supposed to be doing—mission statements should be updated every five years or so. Your statement is a defense against being "unable to see the forest for the trees."

Setting Measurable Objectives

From your mission statement, set some short-term and long-term goals. Consider expressing them by measurable objectives, such as the following:

1. If you are selling all that you make, make increased production an objective—set goals of making "x" more product for the next three years (as a percentage increase over the previous year's production)
2. If you are carrying a lot of inventory, focus on increasing sales—set sales goals for the next three years (as a percentage increase over the previous year's sales)
3. To increase prices—be sure to include by how much and when the increase will occur
4. To create new sources of revenue—be specific about the new products, new outlets, or new services

After setting your short- and long-term objectives, look at them and see if any—particularly long-term goals—can be broken down into measurable mini-goals that are smaller steps to the greater objective. Having measurable objectives allow you to regularly evaluate your progress and, if you fail to achieve any goals, to look into what is preventing you from reaching them. When you do meet your objectives, you can take pride in the achievement, and this can be very important. Making a success of your business is a lot of work, especially for artists who are often not inclined to the rigours of effective business practice, so celebrating milestones of accomplishment often helps you to keep going.

Ways to Grow Your Business

If you really want to make more money from your art, and if you have true talent—in the studio (creative talent) or in business (marketing/promotion talent)—you need more time to devote to the achievement of your objectives. The first questions that can arise are: Where is the time going to come from? From you only? By playing less? By reducing time spent on non-creative work (taking a risk)? By getting a partner or family members to provide you with free labour? By taking on staff, an apprentice, or a volunteer, either full- or part-time? By having "trade" days? (Trade days are when another artist or artists come to your aid for a fixed period of time in exchange for you providing equal time back to each of them.)

If you have lots of inventory or can produce it quickly, your objective may involve selling more of what you have to existing customers by having a sale, increasing contact with your customers, or getting your work into more outlets (market penetration). Alternatively, if you seek new customers by undertaking a sales initiative in a new market (geographic, linguistic, age, religious, etc.), you are undertaking "market expansion."

If you are selling all you make, you will want a business objective that increases inventory—either more of your existing inventory or through the introduction of new products and/or services. If you choose to introduce new products, will they be uniquely different products at the same price point? Can you derive prints from paintings, cards from prints, or use all of or parts of your work to create a design for T-shirts or scarves? To provide a new service, can you teach workshops or offer other new services? Be creative about your business development as you think not only about new products and services, but also about how you will sell any new products you introduce. If you are already selling, will your new products be sold at the same outlets? Consider the time implications of each development objective in order to make the best marketing decisions to create growth in your business.

Market Salons

Market salons are for artists who want to increase sales, source new outlets, find new marketing ideas, or improve on their sales strategies. They are excellent for artists new to sales, beginning their careers, or developing new products or designs. Market salons are successful for graphic artists as well as fine artists, photographers, and crafts persons–anyone with a commercial practice. For neutral, professional marketing feedback, nothing beats a market salon.

Good market salons provide for fifteen minutes per presenting artist and have a knowledgeable facilitator with experience in art sales. A salon for six artist presenters (a two-hour session), for example, allows six artists to register as participants. Another group of artists (no more than ten) register as guests (other artists invited by the presenters and/or participants wanting to witness a salon prior to participating as a registered artist). The presenters have up to five minutes to introduce the work they have brought to the salon (one to three images), leaving ten minutes for feedback.

In their five–minute introduction, presenters address such things as:

1. Their professional experience—their career track (academic/commercial/both); their career level (beginner to seasoned professional).
2. Their sales experience—past sales record, average prices, sales outlets.
3. Where they see their presented piece(s) being sold.
4. An estimate of the price(s) of their piece(s).
5. What kind of specific feedback they are seeking (e.g., where to sell, how to sell, an evaluation).

The facilitator ensures each presenter is limited to fifteen minutes. Any presenter wanting attendees to evaluate the fair market value of their piece(s) can pass around a paper to record the estimates. It's a great idea to have coffee and a snack available after the session for informal discussion if time allows.

Direct Marketing

Direct marketing is advertising directly to the consumer, as opposed to mass marketing practices such as media advertisements. It can be unsolicited or by permission; it can be personalized (the marketing materials bearing the consumer's name), unaddressed, or sent "to the householder." Sometimes direct marketing materials are welcomed by recipients; this is the kind of direct marketing artists need to undertake. As a creative person, you have the capacity to make your print and digital communications more visually appealing—add compelling text and/or irresistible prices to dynamic design to create advertising material that engages recipients.

Direct marketing involves the circulation of a single deliverable, such as an invitation to your exhibition, sale, or open studio. Artists, like other resourceful small businesspersons, find that direct mail is, by far, their most effective sales tool. Direct marketing to a self-made mailing list is the most cost-efficient method of marketing available to you. Nothing beats it!

The Mailing List

Other than having a price rationale, the other essential practice to undertake is the development of a well-coded mailing list. Finding customers is like making friends. You are establishing a relationship with your current and potential buyers, so communicating with them is very important.

Today's software allows you to easily maintain a database, making "personal" communication very easy and effective. With a little time and learning, you can write personalized letters to different categories of friends who are coded into groups on your mailing list—in mass communications, you can address buyers by name, and even mention the titles of their past purchases, for example. Using electronic database- or communication-management software allows you to personalize communications so effectively the recipient will not know you are using a form (or generic) letter.

Creating a database so that you can merge text documents with selected entries on the list is easy for the logical mind, but the artistic person may find this a bit of a challenge. The software should have a print or online reference manual, but you may want to have a friend or paid advisor help you establish your system; maintenance of the database and learning how to use it can be much easier when a professional helps get you started and is available for advice. (As a rule of thumb, it is also a good idea to use software that a friend uses so that you can ask that person for help and advice.)

When you set up your database, you must know how you are going to use it. You must be able to use it selectively, that is, to send mailings to selected categories of listings, so it is very important to code every entry in your list. Some names may have more than one code.

The following is a list of categories of codes used by Marlene:

- Personal (family and friends): F
- Artists (peers): P
- Artists working in the same medium (as Marlene): A
- Galleries: G
- Curators and collectors: C
- Buyers: B
- Potential buyers/exhibition attendees: S
- Miscellaneous: O
- Suppliers: X
- For media, Marlene uses the following codes:
- Vancouver media: LM
- British Columbian (non-Vancouver) media: PM
- Canadian (non-BC) media: CM
- Websites: W

To the above media codes, she adds secondary codes:

- TV: 1
- Radio: 2
- Newspaper: 3
- Magazine: 4
- Corporate communications: 5

It is easy for Marlene to enter names. She has created an interface that makes it simple, but it is because she uses sophisticated software (Filemaker Pro). Spreadsheet programs can work, and there are simple software programs that handle mailing list management. A good program allows you to "merge" a form letter with your database so that your letters can be personally addressed to the people on your mailing list.

SALUTATION	Ms.		
SURNAME	West		
FIRST NAME	Gloria		
ADDRESS 1	#707 — 1177 Hornby Street		
ADDRESS 2			
CITY	Vancouver		
PROV	BC	CODE	V6Z 2E9
PHONE	FIELD 9	EMAIL	------@shaw.ca
PRIME CODE	C, F	CODES 2	
SALES VOL.	$1,260	# OF SALES	3

CODES

F	Personal	LM	Vancouver media
P	Artists (peers)	PM	Provincial media
A	Graphite artists	CM	Canadian media
G	Galleries	W	Websites
C	Curators/ollectors	1	TV
B	Buyers	2	Radio
S	Potential buyers	3	Newspaper
S	Exhibition attendees	4	Magazines
O	Out of town	5	Corporate
X	Suppliers		

BUYS "Nakusp Storm" bought 2001. "Interior Landscape" bought in 2003 ...
"Forgot Myself" bought for their Whistler cabin in 2006. ...

NOTES 2 Gloria bought her pieces from my show in White Rock; buyers M. Mallbank and K. Whiting are her friends and bought from me due to Goria's influence. Gloria's husband is Mark; Charlie and Danielle are her kids.

Figure 6.1. An entry in Marlene's database

Figure 6.1 shows that an entry in Marlene's database has lots of room for information about Gloria West, who is identified as a curator (C) as well as a personal contact (F) in the prime code field.

For each category of contacts, Marlene has a communication strategy:

1. She produces digital newsletters each May and November. They go to most of her mailing list categories—F, P, A, G, C, B, S, X, and O. (Print versions go to those without email.)
2. If she has a show, invitations go by email to the same codes as the digital newsletter. She also sends a very chatty and informal generic letter to her buyers (codes F, P, B, and A) prior to the Christmas season when she always has a sale.
3. She sends birthday cards featuring her art to the people with codes F, P, B, and A.
4. She telephones all her code Bs every spring (May) to invite them to her studio to see her new work. There are no sales ever on this open studio day (because they precede her annual late-spring exhibition), but she will take note of any interested buyers, telling them when her show opens and where it occurs. For the event, she

> hires a caterer and has music playing, creating a party-like atmosphere. The open studio day is for "giving back" to her supporters and developing her most important professional relationships.

For her regular (non-open studio) shows, Marlene creates digital invitations that, of course, feature an image of her work. To create her personalized invitations, she writes a generic letter in her word-processing software that she merges with her mailing list. She writes a generic letter for friends, family, and past buyers, a different letter for those whom she has mailed in the past, and another letter for new people on her list. She then cuts and pastes each personalized letter from her merged documents into an email, attaches her graphic (as a PDF file), and sends off the email. Her email invitations to her friends are very warm and informal; her invites to the galleries and curators are in the more formal language of the visual arts; and she moves to the language of "hype" for her emails to the media. This ability to direct the message in the right language to subgroups of her mailing list is why coding of every entry on your list is so important.

Marlene's database is simple and her use of it is modest compared to other artists who have a great number of categories per product price point or market location. Some artists create different codes for buyers of different kinds of inventory and different volumes of sales. Marlene is about to start producing limited edition prints; the buyers (and potential buyers) of her prints will be coded differently from the buyers of her canvases. In moving into the print market, she is aiming to expand her business to include buyers at a lower price point.

The larger your list, the better your marketing tool. Also, you vastly increase the interest of galleries if you can offer a large and well-made database as part of your promotional tools. How you manage your list will determine how effective it will be—too much communication will turn people off; communicating honestly, infrequently, creatively, and personally can mean increased sales as your list grows. Your list can be augmented by collecting names of people you meet from your travels, from research, and from guest books at your exhibitions—there is no end to how you can collect names. But you should only add good names—names of strategically chosen people or corporations who you really believe may become a buyer. Don't buy names, and use the notes section often to record valuable information about each contact as you learn about them.

Target Marketing

Increasing market penetration or market expansion first involves knowing your customer. Do you have a "typical" customer? Is there a discernable core group in your customer base—be they young people, other artists, women, rich people, or sophisticated buyers? What characteristics dominate your customer profile? How many of your customers are local and how many are tourists? Are all your buyers your friends and/or family? Getting to know your customers—how they found you and what they want—will help you make decisions as to where and how to market and what language to use in your communications. Customer analysis also allows you to know where to find more customers of a similar demographic profile.

A target market is a group of customers who might want your products and services, can afford to purchase them, and are willing and able to buy from you. Many small business owners recognize two types of target markets: individuals and businesses. Typically, individuals make purchases for their own consumption and businesses make purchases that go into the development of value-added products or for re-sale. Artists often do business with other businesses, such as dealers and commercial galleries, owners of corporate collections, and hotels and restaurants (that so often buy art as décor or accept artwork on consignment to place on their walls). Most of the business of contemporary artists, however, is with individual buyers.

Many artists come with their own array of target markets, which in general, are composed in four categories—personal, professional, location, and identity:

1. Personal market: family, friends, neighbours, or peers with whom they regularly communicate.
2. Professional market: doctors, dentists, hairdressers, lawyers, real estate agents, accountants, tradesmen with whom they do business, past buyers, or their own professional affiliations (for those artists with jobs).

3. Location market: where they live, vacation regularly, travel, or where relatives live.
4. Identity market: their linguistic group, church group, sports team, or nationality organization.

You can create your own specific product(s) for a target (or niche) market available to you. If you create a good product for a target market that has an accessible communications medium, such as a professional or identity market, you can easily access new clients through the affiliated organizations' newsletters, websites, professional publications, church bulletins, fax broadcast lists, or at their regular meetings. Also, look for trade publications, trade shows, conventions, and community groups with large memberships such as country clubs, yacht clubs, and golf clubs for marketing and product development opportunities. And think of any other applicable

Example: Mary

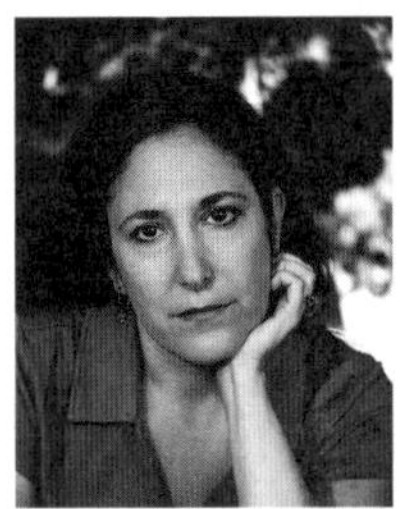

Mary got a commission to do some work for a doctor. A business relationship grew out of their transaction because Mary did far more than was expected of her and it impressed her client. Many years later, when she mentioned she had fallen on tough financial times, the doctor offered to help. He proposed paying for an advertisement in his professional journal that went to thousands of physicians if she could develop what he felt was a "sure sell" product. Mary responded by creating two products: the first, a 200-print edition of a work that included text from the Hippocratic Oath that was a very contemporary design; the second, a 100-print edition of a very traditional "kitchy" work (Mary's adjective) in the style of Norman Rockwell (which she did not like but thought might sell well). The doctor placed the ad in the journal and both prints sold very well as a result of the marketing. Mary also offered to sell them as framed prints, which increased the net profit of many sales. By offering the framing option, Mary took advantage of another marketing trick: value enhancement. Her prints became far more valuable to her customers. They could hang her images right away (instant gratification) and the matting and framing decisions were done for them (work reduction). And, she added twice the cost of the frame to the price of her prints so the profit-per-piece rose.

markets like collectors, pet owners, restaurants doing renovations, interior design firms, fishers—any and every trade or profession—there are many, many niche markets. Niche product development and marketing may seem strange (or commercial) to you at first, but they have a strong advantage—there is little competition from other artists, and this is a business, not a reflection of your core artistic values.

Example: Tom

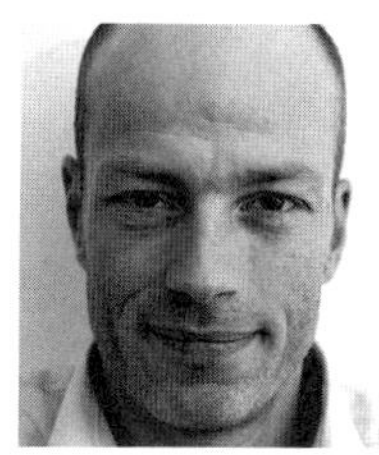

Tom is a very successful painter and art teacher. He publishes instructional books, makes instructional videos, leads workshops, and is excellent at self-promotion. He also loves golf, so as he tours, he offers golf courses a deal: he plays for free and, in exchange, he paints one hole of the course and gives the painting to the golf course. He then partners with the gift shop to sell lithographic offset prints of the painting to members, guests, and vacationing tourists.

Increasing Prices

Successful business development requires a good pricing strategy. The right price covers all true costs of creating your product, as well as a fair profit, and is acceptable to the consumer. Pricing is an art and a science—it is part materials and creation time, part reputation or status, and part "what the market will bear." It involves researching your market and the prices of peers ("competitors").

What assumptions do you make about a lawyer whose fee is $30 per hour versus a lawyer whose fee is $1000 per hour, or about a $15 meal versus a $120 meal? Pricing involves perceived value as well as the customer's ability and willingness to pay. The difference between perceived value and price can often motivate buyers—when customers feel that your price is below market value, they feel that they are getting a bargain; a perception that a product is overpriced will kill consumer interest.

Increasing your prices is part of keeping a good inventory diary. Price increases should be infrequent and justified by career milestones recorded in your diary. (*See chapter two for more information on an inventory diary or to help you make your pricing decisions.*)

Packaging

Part of your product is its package, and packaging should be part of your mix of marketing materials. In the contemporary marketplace in Vancouver, there is, for example, a tremendous "green" consciousness. If your work is on hand-made paper, or acid-free paper, or your work uses recycled materials, or if you are using recycled paper—any and all of these things can add value to your work, and such information would be valuable on the packaging or labeling of your work.

Most of us rely on labeling when we buy food—just as you look at the ingredients of what you eat, your buyers will appreciate your providing them with information on your media. Ingredients of much of contemporary art can deteriorate over time, depending on the conditions of where it is shown or stored. Your buyers need to know what you use in order that they can effectively protect it. One aspect of packaging that is clever is including instructions on how to take care of your work. By giving unexpected yet considerate, valuable, and free information to your buyers, you get loyalty, respect, and often, return business.

For the unrepresented artist, another aspect of effective packaging is the provision of biographical information. This can mean nothing more than providing a website or blog address on your label or sales tag. A corollary of art sales is that knowledgeable buyers invest in the artist; they do not just buy art. (*See the Sales Tags section of chapter eight for more about the importance of biographical information with sales.*)

Perhaps the most important aspect of packaging, when it comes to works of art on paper, is framing. Framing can protect the work when done correctly (*see chapter fifteen*) as well as enhance the presentation of the work. Creating your work on paper of standard sizes allows you to save money on framing because you can buy manufactured frames off the shelf instead of requiring a custom frame.

Personal Selling

The "call to action" of the marketing campaigns of most contemporary artists is to attend a sale or an exhibition opening. At these events, artists' marketing campaigns shift from indirect (e.g., mailed or emailed communication or advertising) to direct, personal promotional techniques.

Personal selling is, by far, the most important and most successful form of marketing for many visual artists/businesspersons. It involves a direct, face-to-face relationship with the customer. It will usually mean explaining your work as part of the effort to persuade your customer to buy it.

Personal contact with artists is often valued by customers who:

1. Are return customers.
2. Bring friends to see your work.
3. Want to meet the artist of works they buy.
4. Are buying art for the first time
5. Feel that your price is high (in terms of their income or the prices of your peers).
6. May want to return your work
7. Want reassurance
8. Want to negotiate

Personal communication produces more sales than any other marketing technique. It is through the establishment of a relationship—even a momentary one—that moves sales. If the customer likes or respects you, interest in your products and services rises. Always be available, warm, open, and honest. (*See the Selling to First-Time Buyers section later in this chapter for more information about personal selling techniques.*)

Personal selling can also be an unpleasant experience for your customers, and, consequently, you or your gallery. If customers do have a negative experience, they are unlikely to patronize you again and will tell others about your failure(s)—always, always be polite and patient with your customers.

As personal selling figures so prominently in the professional practice of artists, it is important to master the art of interpersonal communications and always be thinking of sales as you lead your daily life. Always remember to collect the contact information of every person you meet who expresses interest in your work, knows of other buyers, is connected to the media, or is part of large communication network—everyone and anyone who might figure in the advancement of your career. Add everyone to your mailing list, appropriately coded. From then on, it's up to you to turn them into customers through your effective, compelling, and not-too-frequent direct marketing practices.

Up-Selling

Up-selling is the adding of value to a sale. When you are selling wares directly to your customers, you have the chance to increase the value of the sale by adding a product or service to the purchase—"Would you like me to arrange for the framing of this piece?" you might ask a buyer of your work for example (following the example of McDonald's "Would you like fries with that order?"). Another up-selling practice is to offer a second painting at half-price or X% off, for example, to friends are shopping together (and who often represent two households).

Up-selling practices, whatever they may be, can be visible or invisible. If they are visible through signs or in sales material (discounts, two-for-one's, extras, or bonuses), they can easily make an artist look too commercial or desperate (and therefore probably not a very good artist). Up-selling is often best used by the artist as an invisible incentive—a sales tool that you or your gallery agents can mention to appropriate potential buyers.

Example: Jane

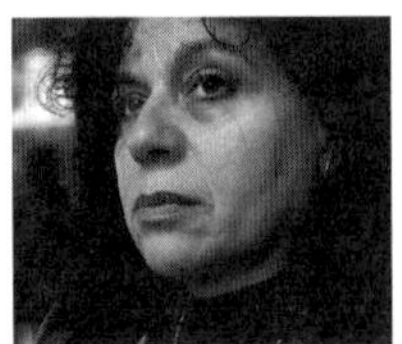

Jane is an artist skilled in up-selling. Her largest works sell for many thousands of dollars. Corporate clients buy most of her work. A few times, however, a corporate purchase has led to a staff member wanting a piece of her work for their home. With all her sales, Jane offers her buyers packages of blank greeting cards with the image of their purchased work on the front. She also offers to have any message that the purchaser wants printed in the cards. This practice has proven very popular with most of her buyers, especially her corporate clients (with large budgets), who often order hundreds to thousands of cards. Jane charges a healthy price for the cards, thereby increasing her profit from the sale. (Jane sometimes provides a modest amount of cards for free to buyers who refer her to others who buy her work.)

Selling to First-Time Buyers

There are many obstacles to buying art for those who have never bought before. First-time buyers may feel insecure, feeling that they do not "understand" art well enough to make a wise purchase and fearing the negative judgment of others for their choices. They may also think that they do not know anything about you, what "good" art is, if your work will last, or what your art is really worth.

> **Example: David**
>
> 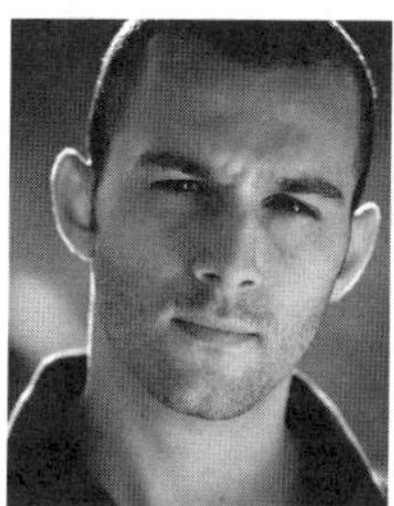
>
> David is a prolific painter who is good at selling his work. He has two prices on his canvases: one higher and one lower. His customers always ask, "Why two prices?" He responds with his business-savvy answer: "You pay the lower price, you take the painting home—end of story. You pay the higher price, and you can come back and trade it in for another piece of the same size or value, once a year for ten years, as long as the work returned is in pristine condition. If you damage a work—you own it forever and no more trade-ins."

You must address these issues when you are dealing with a first-time, reluctant, or nervous buyer. You must exude your worthiness; you have to remove their concerns. You can address first-time buyers' jitters in several ways:

1. Congratulate them on their decision to buy original art; tell them how your work will address their desires.
2. Show them your portfolio.
3. Provide details about your most prestigious collectors/buyers from your updated list of buyers.
4. Mention your other favourable experiences with first-time buyers.
5. Show them your reviews and publicity in your portfolio (but not outdated ones!).
6. Explain that you use a price rationale to ensure the ongoing market value of your work (making it a safe investment).

7. Talk about any exhibition experience, awards, and/or commissions of significance—drop any names you can without being boring or obvious (subtlety is good!).
8. Ask where they would put your piece in their home or office and offer ideas about presentation.
9. Talk about conservation: tell them why your work will not fade or decay.
10. Offer to deliver and help install your work.
11. Offer to let them take it home on a trial basis if you trust them or if they leave a deposit (always check their ID and make note of all their contact information).
12. Give them your contact information.

People need support in making big purchases, not just when they buy art. Listen to them, look at them in the eye when you are speaking and listening; be courteous and helpful. Use appropriate language; do not use "artspeak" with first-time buyers. Be helpful and encouraging.

When Times are Tough

When times are tough for everyone and not just you—when there is a recession or depression, or when unemployment rates are high—artists can have noticeable difficulties with sales. At these times, when people are getting laid off, taking cuts in pay or losing jobs to downsizing or bankruptcies, you may have to drop your prices. If your sales are down, if fewer people are responding to your invitations, if your gallery is finding the sale of work down for all their artists, drop your prices, offer to be paid in installments, or offer exchanges (making note of all the reasons for you price reductions in your pricing diary). Some artists become entrepreneurial during such times, producing work that is inexpensive and about the economic challenges of the times, or producing optimistic, powerful statements.

An "emergency" sale is creditable if there is a crisis in your life. When you are faced with real adversity, a sale to raise "emergency" revenue can be very effective. This is a practice that should be done rarely. At such a time (serious illness, studio fire, relocation), reduce prices and develop an invitation and/or sales flyer that can communicate with a large number of people on your mailing list. Your notice should focus on the need for "inventory reduction" (tell them why) and provide examples of your "highly discounted" prices. Don't sell your best work at these events—hide it. Use the sale to move pieces that have not sold over time, multiples, slightly damaged work, and/or those pieces that no longer represent your artistic voice.

Diversifying Productivity

One important aspect of effective marketing and small business management is to know "what" to market as much as "how" to market. As a business concerned with making a profit, sometimes instead of increasing the time, energy, and money you put into selling the work that you do, an investment in new artistic products or services is the best route to the growth of your business. You may be able to derive new products for the general marketplace from the work you do as an artist—especially if you create work for which a market already exists (e.g., landscapes, animal portraits, florals, or character studies). Or, you may want to create work specifically for an available target market.

> ### Example: Simon
>
> 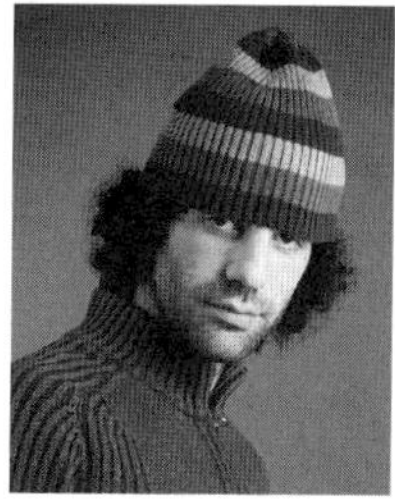
>
> Simon paints in acrylics. His artistic career is a sideline occupation because he lives in a small community, but his work is popular with residents and with tourists who visit his town in the summertime. When the town's only large employer, a lumber mill, closed ten years ago, Simon lost his job along with most of the town's residents. As Christmas time approached, he held a sale in the community hall, but instead of dropping prices, he offered a second small painting to every buyer of his "regular" work, and this sales strategy worked very well. Rather than drop his prices at a time when he needed money, he added value and maintained his income level from making art.

Your decision as to whether to invest in new products or services may depend on how much extra time will be required for creation, additional administration, and marketing, as well as how much money you have to invest in new inventory and marketing materials.

You may, for example, be able to rent your work that is not selling or that you do not want to sell. Or you may be able to derive prints from your paintings, as well as posters or cards. The ideal is to have a product line (a variety of inventory) for your business that has several price points (like packaged cards at $20, small prints at $125, large prints at $300, and paintings at $1000), keeping in mind that the lesser the investment of time and money in product development, the greater the potential for profit. The

Example: Bryan

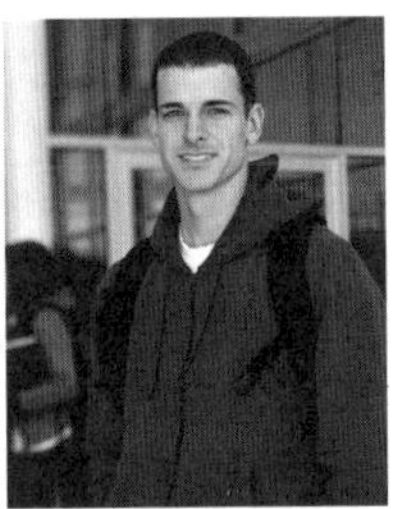

Bryan creates elaborate stencils that he uses to create designs on paper. Each year, his stencils are all related—shapes of leaves, toys, tools, flowers, cars—and his palette changes with every series. He uses the six to ten stencils that he makes each year to make original "prints" of an infinite variety. Each one is different and completely original, but they share a relationship. His clients can also design their own original as a commission, telling Bryan what palette and stencils they like. He does not, however, earn enough money so he increased awareness of his services and products by having a booth at the annual "home design" show in his hometown. Several interior designers saw his work, including Aaron who wholesales products to designers and retail outlets. Aaron ordered a custom design from Bryan and had it lithographed as a poster. It sold well, so his next order was for two more prints that also were turned into posters.

Aaron has diversified the application of Bryan's designs. Besides the posters, Aaron is publishing cards and stationery from Bryan's designs, and clients can order an original from the current year (or from any past years) through Aaron's website. And through all the growth, Bryan's basic work has not changed—he is still making the six to ten stencils each year. From a dozen simple designs, Bryan and Aaron create a diverse array of products at different price points (both retail and wholesale) that fit into a distribution network that Aaron has created over time. And due to Aaron's work, Bryan is far better known, his annual exhibitions have moved to a larger venue and his sales have grown significantly.

items in your product line must have aesthetic and qualitative consistencies, and you must develop a business reputation of promptness, fairness, diversity, and excellence in design.

Offering Services

Besides the diversification of products, artists can consider offering services. There are many possibilities, including renting out studio space, teaching workshops (at a regional college, community centre, or through a local arts council or organization), offering consultation services (to other artists, interior designers, teachers, or homeowners), or offer writing services (reviewing shows for local media, writing artist statements for other artists, or writing for other galleries).

Example: Guy

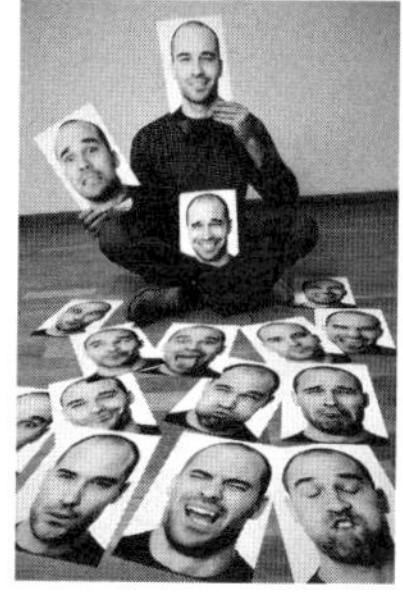

Guy is a photographer who makes collages of transparencies that mix his own images with images appropriated from magazine advertising. When Guy moved to a new apartment shared with two other artists, they had only one bathroom. The bathtub had a glass sliding door that closed to create the shower enclosure. His roommates wanted something done to the glass to make it opaque so that people could use the facilities while someone showered. Guy used a transfer technique to lift images of rivers and waterfalls from old magazines onto Mylar. He then collaged the transparent lifts onto the outside of the glass and then he covered his assemblage with self-adhesive Mylar. His designs looked like a giant collage slide transparency.

The parents of one of Guy's roommates asked Guy to do the same thing to their bathroom doors, but sandwiching the images between sheets of glass. When the glass door manufacturer, Acer Glass, came to install the glass, the company owner arranged to meet Guy. Acer Glass now offers Guy's services as an option to all their clients. Success can happen by accident! (When Guy established his relationship with Acer Glass, he adapted his work to recognize the copyrights of the images he used.)

Ingenuity, creativity, entrepreneurialism—whatever you call it—if you have it, diversifying your output may come easily. If you cannot see how you can diversify, consult with other artists. There is no end to the possibilities. Creativity is as vital a tool for your business decisions as it is in the creative decisions you make every day in your studio.

SEVEN

Marketing on the Internet

"When my daughter was about seven years old, she asked me one day what I did at work. I told her I worked at the college—that my job was to teach people how to draw. She stared at me, incredulous, and said, 'You mean they forget?'" —*Howard Ikemoto*

"Absolutely nothing has had a more positive impact on my career than the Internet. I find self-promotion and marketing infinitely easier and more efficient now that I have a website and a couple of blogs. You can communicate text, moving and still images, and sound in far-reaching campaigns, all from your own studio/office." —*C. T.*

The Artist as Investment

There are many visually astute buyers who think and act as investors in the artist rather than mere buyers of their work. As an investor, they want to stay informed of the artist and his or her practice. They want to know the basic profile of who the artist is and the nature of her or his artistic drive, and they want to know about the artist's trends, interests, themes, and goals. Nothing better affords the fulfillment of the buyers' desire to know about the artist than an artist's website and/or blog. The Internet affords a tremendous medium for self-promotion.

The Benefits of the Internet

There are many benefits of marketing and selling artwork via the Internet, specifically in regards to market research, market expansion, sales support, customer service, and marketing costs.

1. Market research: The many artists' websites make it easy for you to research pricing, website design, and sales outlets. Chat groups for visual artists can provide easy marketing answers and resources, as well as a community of peers. Also, modest market research can be conducted by email polling of people on your mailing list.
2. Market expansion: Artists, particularly those with specialties, can benefit from the international market the Internet affords; they can rapidly expand their mailing lists through online research.
3. Sales support: Buyers can learn more about you, your techniques, creative mission, and the materials you use, and they can learn how to properly frame and maintain artwork, for example, from your website or blog.
4. Customer service: You can easily maintain the relationship with your buyers via email, and your clients can easily find and contact you with questions or requests for more work.
5. Marketing costs: Communication expenses can be reduced and targets can be expanded using the Internet instead of the postal system or other avenues of communication.

Your Internet Investment

A web presence is a valuable professional development asset—especially now that so many sites offer free blog space. And, many Internet service providers—such as Shaw, Rogers, and Telus in Canada—provide modest website hosting capacity to their customers as part of their service package. With modest technological skills, this is a good option for artists wanting simple Internet exposure.

The Internet is also highly effective for both image and sound transmission—it serves installation and performance artists particularly well. Your use of these technologies as self-promotion tools and/or an e-gallery will be as effective as your skills permit, unless you hire professional website development services. Proficiency in software, possession of technological tools (like a digital camera, scanner, and digital sound recorder and/or video camera), and healthy financial resources are all factors affecting your capacity to take full advantage of the Internet.

If you do not have the tools and skills with which to create and maintain a blog and/or website, or if you do not have the time it takes to have and maintain (update) an effective presence on the Internet, hire a professional to help you. A site that does not change regularly or does not give visitors a feeling that it is an integral part of your artistic practice is a weak site. An effective web presence requires an ongoing investment of time; if you do not have the time to devote to its maintenance, again, hire a professional. (Or better yet, find a professional who will trade his/her services for some of your art.)

An alternative route to an Internet presence is to take advantage of websites offering promotional/marketing services to visual artists—but only deal with reputable sites—there are many that exist to serve the site owner rather than the artist/clients. My Art Club (myartclub.com) and ArtSites (ArtSites.ca) are two Canadian visual art web-service sites that enjoy a good reputation. Whether your build your website yourself, hire a professional to do it for you, or if you become part of an online visual artists' community, you must know what you want from the Internet, and why you are investing in it.

Setting Goals

Do you want to sell or just inform on the Internet? Do you want interaction or a more passive presence? Are you prepared for a lot of web maintenance time or do you only want to do biannual or annual updates? If you want to sell products or services, you will have to present an inventory of your products and services that may require constant to infrequent maintenance, depending on the nature of your artistic business practice. And you will have to deal, one way or another, with the complex issues of credit card sales, shipping, and taxation. (E-commerce is a time-consuming, costly, and demanding aspect of website development—the alternative is to use PayPal.) If your site is going to be an informational one with referral contact information for sales, what image do you want to create? What emotion do you want to evoke? How do you want to present yourself? What is the right tone of language to use?

Assess your competency. Can you do the writing your blog or website will require? Can you create effective and compelling graphics? Are you able to design to create the tone and atmosphere you want? Do you have the time and skills to do all these things well? Should you engage professional help in any of these areas?

By far, the most popular use of the Internet by artists is marketing by email, which is also their primary method of advertising. Blogs are also a favourite of artists. Blogs began as e-diaries, but their use has grown to also become the "poor man's website" because it is hosted for free. Another "poor man's" Internet marketing strategy is to have a modest website hosted by your Internet service provider that links to your blog that is hosted by a free site. This way, your images, that are often larger files, are residing on your blog, not your website server. Some artists use sites such as Flicker to host their images, providing links to those images from their blog and website.

But the most dynamic Internet presence—one that can take best advantage of search engines—is the professional website designed for your all your marketing and sales needs. If you are building your own site, you will need a lot of skills, software, and equipment; if you are buying website building and design services, the person you hire should help you set clear objectives for the site.

Visit the site of other artists to help you determine what it is you want to do. There are lots of them and they are easy to find (such as the previously mentioned My Art Club and ArtSites).

Internet-Use Models

You can consider two models of Internet-use for artists: one for increasing sales revenue and one for increasing your profile.

With the first model, creating a new revenue stream via the Internet requires that you, on the high end, create a secure website capable of handling sales transactions or is linked to transaction services such as PayPal. Also, you will have to maintain a marketing campaign that drives visitors to your site. On the low end, you have (or buy) the graphic skills required to use email as a marketing tool or for research and/or to maintain a blog.

The second model involves using the Internet as a self-promotional and communications tool that focuses on creating an entertaining, easy-to-use information-based website. Ideally, it features specialized marketing programs, such as featured products or services (e.g., artwork of the month, season, or year); information about upcoming exhibitions, sales, or open studio days; "special" Internet pricing on selected (or all) of your inventory; this month's favourite links (or another strategy that brings visitors back to your site); or a monthly or seasonal editorial, column, letter, or blog entry (perhaps a gallery visit diary with photos of openings you attend and admire).

Generating Visits to Your Website

Websites do very little without support. People will not visit your site unless you entice them with emails, advertising, or publicity. The most

Example: MJ

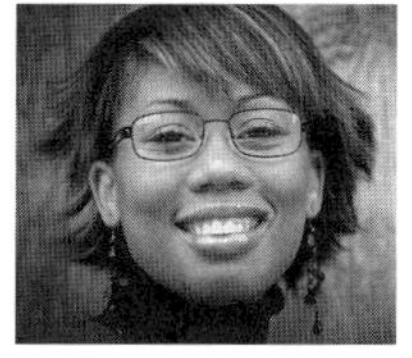

MJ is a printmaker. Every quarter, she emails all the people on her list, announcing her new works. MJ is an astute artist because she has a small list of names and she takes the time to personalize an email to each one. Also, she places a unique number on each email and she advises all her email recipients that one of the numbers earns the holder a free etching if they visit her website. Her offer inspires most of the people on her list to visit her site to see if they have won the print. Once there, everyone who does not have the winning number are invited to have 25% off any purchase over $200.

important part of planning your website is your strategy for driving people to your site (unless it is to be a passive informational site that serves to support your face-to-face or direct mail marketing initiatives). You must plan what you are going to do, and at what cost, to drive visitors—especially new visitors—to your site.

"Tagging" each of your images with your name is important. The more images you tag, the more accessible you are on the web—search engines seek tags.

Example: David

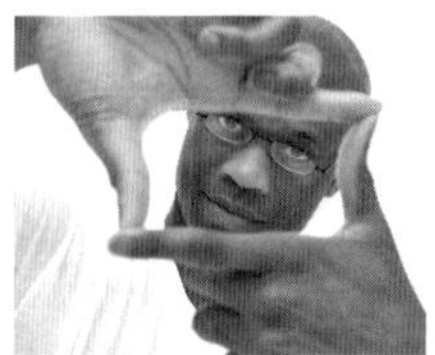

David is an artist who got into a habit of keeping a diary in his studio in which to record pigment ratios, sources of collage materials, and other details pertinent to the development of his work. He often referred to his diary in conversation with his gallery and some buyers. This led his gallery to suggest that he transfer his diary information on each piece onto a blog. He now jokingly refers to himself as the "cabbage patch artist" because each piece he makes has its own story on his blog. The owner of the gallery representing David values the blog as a sales tool. He says buyer interest has been extremely positive—so positive that he is advising other artists to follow the same practice.

A website provides interested parties with an opportunity to access deep insights into your work and career. Your business card can open the door to your heart and soul by simply listing your URL. The following sections provide practical tips on getting a website started either on your own or in the company of a website designer or builder.

Plan Your Site

Decide what the main sections of the site will be. Then, make a list of these primary sections of the site. Below is a plan for a simple, fourteen-page website; each box represents a page and the boxes below are a breakdown of that page's content.

My Web Plan

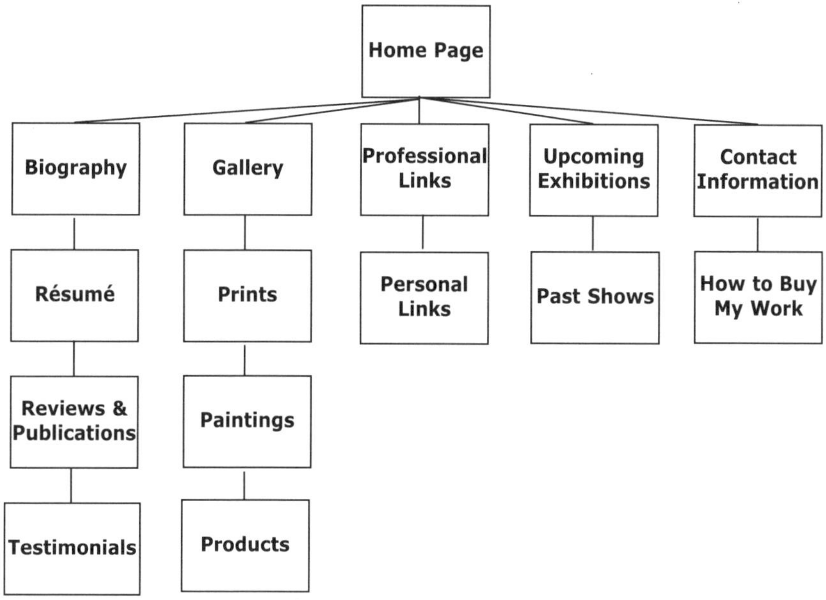

Figure 7.1. Peter's website plan

Home Page: includes a favourite image and quote about being creative (which Peter can frequently update); music automatically starts when the user logs onto the site; there are also navigation tools to the website's sections.

Biography: has a different image, plus a short biography and a photo of Peter; there are navigation icons to his résumé, reviews, and testimonials by his buyers.

Gallery: contains his artist statement, plus another representational image; there are navigation icons to his Prints, Paintings, and Product sub-pages that serve as a visual record of his past exhibitions presented graphically (as opposed to them in written form in his résumé).

Professional Links: contains interesting statistics about life as an artist in Canada, drawn from information provided by Statistics Canada, plus links to Peter's professional organizations (e.g., CARFAC, the Vancouver Alliance for Arts and Culture, and the Malaspina Printmakers). Its

Personal Links page provides an annotated list of websites that he likes: sites by other artists, favourite Mac computer-support sites, favourite films on YouTube, his blog, other blogs, Facebook info, et cetera.

Upcoming Exhibitions: this section focuses on Peter's ideas and objectives as an artist, presented in the context of his upcoming and past exhibitions. On these pages, he tells visitors of his exhibition achievements (artistically as well as in terms of attendance, contacts, and sales). He also describes the host gallery and expresses thanks and praise for organizers, staff, and volunteers. These pages are illustrated with representational images but are not a complete visual record of the work; he lists the pieces shown in each exhibition, and if you click on each title, it links you to the image in the Gallery section.

An important note: All the images you use on the web should be low resolution and watermarked. "Watermarking" involves altering the image with a transparent mark that interferes with the image. Your mark may or may not include the copyright symbol, but the purpose of watermarking is to protect your image from unauthorized reproduction.

Contact Page: this page is straightforward. It contains all Peter's contact information: blog address, email address, cell phone, studio phone number, and retail sales outlets (but no street or studio addresses). On his How to Buy My Work page, he explains why he does not want to be represented by a gallery—astutely mentioning that his policy affords buyers lower prices since he does not pay any commissions. A How to Buy button on the contact page reveals a form that can be emailed to Peter so he can contact the buyer directly to complete the sale.

Collect Your Data

Before building your site or having it built, collect all your data. Gather digital images (in the right format) for the gallery and exhibitions sections and all the text required. Your biography, résumé, artist statement, reviews and publications, any sound clips, animations, or films and testimonials—get it all together. And consider having a professionally shot portrait for your biography page. Be sure to factor in potential navigational issues and downloading time in your planning. If any part of these website tips are incomprehensible to you, and unless you have strong technological skills, hire a professional designer—one who will construct a site and train you to do easy and constant maintenance.

Things to remember when building your website:

1. **Choose a domain name.** You must search for, register, and pay for the rights to use your domain name. Have options, as many domain names are already taken, and keep its name very simple. For many artists, "yourname.com" has proven effective, as it is just about always available and easy to remember.
2. **Get a host.** Your host is where the files of your website reside for access by Internet users. Use the web space provided by your Internet supplier or have a contract with a hosting company by the month, year, or multi-year payment package. The fee for hosting is based on the size (the amount of bytes) of your site. Fees also are affected by whether or not you incorporate other available services (such as an email address or password) in the architecture of your site. The amount of space offered by Internet service providers such as Shaw and Rogers is usually enough for a basic artist's website. The website addresses that they offer you, however, are cumbersome, so you may not want to use their services. (The sites *register.com*, *readyhosting.com*, or *godaddy.com* offer domain-name registration and provide hosting services.) Google "website hosting" and search Canadian pages to learn more about website hosts available to you.
3. **Be organized** before designing and building the site. An outline of the site's pages and sections (like figure 7.1) and the corresponding data are the tools you and/or your designer needs to begin construction. Know the colour palette you want to use and the "feel" you want to provide viewers. If you engage a professional designer and do not know whom to choose, try contacting an artist in your area (whose site you like) to see if the artist will give you the name and contact information of the web designer. Also, arts schools, Craigslist, and artist organizations may be valuable resources to help you identify a designer appropriate to your needs.

Students of design schools will often provide services at reduced rates; some artists are successful in trading art for web design and construction services.

The following are some helpful online web-design resources:

- *jessett.com* and *tizag.com*—primers for creating websites
- *webstyleguide.com* and *webrightnow.com*—instructional sites on creating websites
- *entheosweb.com*—free instruction with an orientation to specific software (Fireworks and Dreamweaver)
- *webdesignfromscratch.com*—comprehensive guide to designing a website
- If you have decent computer skills and a good how-to book, you can construct a website with the appropriate software. These programs enable you to create and manage your website with little HTML knowledge:
- Adobe GoLive (*adobe.com/products/golive*)
- Microsoft FrontPage: (*microsoft.com/frontpage*)
- Adobe (Macromedia) Dreamweaver (*adobe.com/products/dreamweaver/*)

If you include images of your artwork on your site, you will also need a good image-editing program, such as Adobe Photoshop Elements (*adobe.com/products/photoshopelwin*). Mac users might also want to look for the shareware program GraphicConverter (*lemkesoft.com*). It converts pictures to different formats and also contains many useful features for picture manipulation.

The two most common image file formats for the web are JPEG and GIF. Use JPEGs for images of artwork and GIFs for buttons and other graphic elements. The resolution of these image files should be no larger than 72 dpi. Any files with a larger dpi will increase the download time for your images. And remember, use low-resolution images and watermark them for security against copyright infringement.

4. **Know the publishing process.** Once your site has been created it needs to be uploaded, or "published," to your host. If this is something your designer does, you should learn how to update and

republish pages of your site so you have independence in keeping your site current. Publishing is an ongoing process as you update pages or make additions to your site—every time you make a change, you have to republish. A file transfer protocol (FTP) program allows you to transfer files from your home computer to your host's server when you need to update your site. Some good FTP programs that are free are Freeware and Shareware (*versiontracker.com* or *webattacl/cp*) and CuteFTP (*cuteftp.com/cuteftp*), a Windows-based FTP application that allows you to utilize the capabilities of FTP without having to know all the protocols.

5. **Make your site easy to find:** If you are building a site to advance sales and income, it is important to ensure that users will be able to easily search for and find your site. You or your web designer must build features into your site to make this happen. For more information on how search engines work and tips for submitting to search engines, visit www.SearchEngineWatch.com.

Email Marketing

Gail has what she calls "reasonable" skills in Photoshop. She is also good with words and has considerable promotional skills. She is personable, and she has a large mailing list. For her, it is easy to create a catching graphic invitation as a PDF file. (PDF files are universally readable. This is important in the visual art world where a disproportionate number of people are on Macintosh computers and not using Microsoft Windows. Also, PDF files can be emailed to print houses for printing, which allows you to support your digital marketing materials with identical hardcopy materials.)

When Gail has a show or event, she makes a PDF file with an eye-popping image plus the essential information of date, place, and time. Then, she writes a personalized form email to her mailing list, attached with the PDF file. She invites her email recipients to circulate her invitation to their friends, inviting them in their own words to attend as well as forwarding them Gail's PDF graphic. This virtually free marketing method is her most efficient and successful way of advertising exhibitions and sales.

This method of marketing is effective only if it is not over used; do this too often, and it will backfire, turning your friends into people who do not want to hear from you. Always include information on how recipients can be removed from your email list.

Evaluation

As with any marketing strategy, the effectiveness of your Internet marketing program should be evaluated. Artists should measure their website performance in terms of achieving the goals set out when they originally planned the site. Has the website had a measurable impact on your business? Does it take too much work to maintain? Is it building your mailing list with buyers, not only bytes? Is it getting lots of visitors? Identify ways to increase traffic to your site if you are not happy with results of your Internet venture, see if things change, and do not be afraid to abandon a site that is not working for you and is costing you hosting fees.

Artists + eBay

When eBay began, there were few categories of visual art and "art" meant anything, from originals to copies of historical works to posters. It was decidedly seller and buyer unfriendly. Now, there are many categories, including one of self-represented artists. But—and this is a big but—inexperienced visitors have trouble finding the appropriate category, and if they do, the searches are organized by the times that the auctions end and they include work from the sublime to the ridiculous. Visual art buyers, therefore, have been unlikely to use the site, and this is too bad because it is a powerful sales tool. The site's potential and problems, however, were not lost on John Seed.

A Californian artist, writer and professor, Seed created an online community of visual artists who use eBay called EBSQ (www.ebsqart.com). It is a member-based, member-run site that began in 2000. Other people now own the site, but it remains an organization dedicated to the self-representing artist—that is, artists without a gallery, dealer, or agent working to further their sales. EBSQ, as you learn on the website, is a name "derived from the [tag] name e-Basquiat." The early members liked Basquiat's work and they self-identified as outsiders—*réfuséé*—of the gallery system and as self-directors of their careers. (Basquiat tagged his work "SAMO.") Whenever reproductions of their work are posted online on eBay, "EBSQ" is in the title line of every piece of art that members post for auction. Using their tag in every title allows visitors to the eBay site to simply search for "EBSQ" in order to receive their choices in art that meet a certain standard.

Originally, ebsqart/com offered free membership to any artist interested in joining; it continues to allow any artist to join, but the site now charges a modest annual fee. Now, it has a juried section called "EBSQ+" that assesses factors such as quality and professionalism; the work of juried members has "EBSQ+" in their title line.

The idea behind this online community is a strength-in-numbers philosophy that allows peer artists to cultivate collectors in a way similar to galleries. Through cooperation, they create a brand that is easy to find on eBay for all who know about EBSQ. And their buyers are saved from viewing countless images of mediocre work.

Any group of artists can follow this model—establishing an online sales presence easily and inexpensively in partnership with an online community of peers. This is a different kind of community than the popular My Art Club and ArtSites, which are excellent for more experienced buyers of more expensive work. eBay works well for relatively inexpensive work for the mass market, and even though it works best for lower priced work, there is no middleman so you pay no commission.

This is certainly something that is not for everyone, but for those who like working online, live in areas without art galleries, and have no representation, eBay can be useful in partnership with a group such as EBSQ.

artistsurvivalskills.com

Updates and corrections to the text of this primer, plus additional relevant material will be posted on the website *artistsurvivalskills.com*.

EIGHT

The Artist's Portfolio & Other Primary Sales Tools

"Creativity is allowing yourself to make mistakes. Art is knowing which ones to keep." —*Scott Adams*

"Luck, personality, business savvy, knowing someone—any number of things can get your foot in the door, but it is your portfolio that determines whether or not you get invited back." —*C. T.*

The Artist's Portfolio

The artist's portfolio is a valuable tool to support the artist's bid for representation, to secure a commission or exhibition, and to promote sales. It is one of the most important tools the artist has to establish a professional relationship, especially since the portfolio is often shown in person, while allowing the artist to elaborate on its contents.

A portfolio contains various presentation materials. Basically, an effective portfolio contains:

1. A résumé and a biography.
2. An artist statement.
3. Samples of work.
4. Press clippings or reviews.
5. A list of collectors and/or commissions and/or awards.

(Sometimes educational and training information is included but this type of information is usually presented in the artist's résumé.) Your portfolio is an ever-changing collection of information—continually refreshed or updated—that can be adapted for specific needs or purposes.

Today, some artists concentrate on electronic sales tools, focusing on an elaborate website instead of the traditional presentation-style portfolio. Having both is ideal, but a three-dimensional portfolio that viewers can touch is essential—websites can be viewed without the artist present and, depending on the calibration of the viewer's monitor, colour reproduction can be haphazard. Artists usually present their portfolio personally, after an initial contact with the viewer by means of a telephone call, letter of introduction, or in response to a call for entry for an exhibition. It is usually being presented to someone who is already, to some extent, interested in your work. It is, therefore, an important sales tool that can make or break the establishment of a business relationship.

Ideally, your portfolio is a nice, clean presentation case (not too large) that is easy to view on a flat surface. All component parts should be clean, not look used or worn, and there should be no spelling or grammatical mistakes in the text. Proofread everything carefully and ask one or more artist friends to review it before you use it.

A common fault with artists' portfolios is the amount of materials many artists include. Be judicious with your selections so that your portfolio is very impressive and there are only enough images to effectively represent the work you want the viewer to see. If you are presenting a portfolio to a curator in hopes of securing an exhibition, do not show all your work—be appropriately selective. It is easy to be selective with your portfolio because you can put everything that is "extra" on your website or blog or you can invite the curator or gallery owner to visit you in your studio. Also, do not repeat information on your website and in your portfolio—doing so sends a bad message to anyone interested enough in your work to pursue both resources (you do not want to waste their time by showing the exact same content on your website as they see in your portfolio). (A website-portfolio hybrid is the portfolio that contains a CD-ROM or DVD that you leave with the appraiser. Again, your CD or DVD should reinforce but not repeat information that is contained in your portfolio and oral presentation.)

Every year, art schools are graduating more and more artists, and every year more and more retirees are making visual art their creative avocation. Competition is increasing for the artist selling in conventional formats and locations. You must stand out by having a portfolio that is somehow unforgettable (artistic talent assumed).

The Résumé & Biography

The artist's résumé is a summary of your artistic experience. It is an opportunity to present your creative achievements in a thoroughly businesslike manner; it is not a place for visual expression. The résumé is a business document and it should be presented in sections: employment history (limited to work related to the visual arts and creativity), exhibition history, corporate and private collections that include your work, commissions, awards, and reviews. Section headings may vary according to your artistic practice, but these sections are basic components in most artists' résumés. Section headings should stand out.

A résumé should be chronological and brief; it is best presented in point form. It should be typed, and it's a good idea to have a longer version (no more than four pages) and a shorter version if you have an extensive history. The résumé should be easy to read (use twelve-point type if possible)—do not use coloured or textured paper—and it focuses on the artist's exhibitions, recognition, and sales achievements. A résumé is different than a curriculum vitae (CV), which focuses on the artist's lifetime education, training, and employment history. A CV usually serves to secure employment rather than an exhibition or a commission; neither is it a biography.

Like all writing, a résumé can be either well done or not. Good writing is a skill. If you are not confident of your writing skills, get help from a friend or from a professional (a technical writer). Also, look at the résumés of other artists—either ask artist friends to show you their résumés or ask a local gallery to share some with you that they have received.

Biographical information is usually provided in a narrative form and in the third-person voice. Biographies provide contextual information about the artist that may include material also present in the résumé (or CV), but they read like a story. Biographies are most often seen in exhibition catalogues, on websites, and in artist books.

The Portrait

Another valuable element of the portfolio is a portrait of the artist. A print portrait should not stand-alone and be large in presentation—a thumbnail-sized portrait as part of the résumé or one that is a modest size as part of your biographical material is ideal. You may want to have more than one form of portrait—one can be a photograph and the other an artistic portrait done by you or another artist. And a portrait is what it should be—a portrait. It should not be a casual snapshot, or part of a snapshot. It should look professional. Save your portrait images in various formats—a TIFF or PDF file, and of sufficient density and size to be effectively reproduced in all forms of print media.

The Artist Statement

The best artist statement is written by the artist and is in the first-person voice. It focuses on the creative process—the inner creative voice of the artist. (Artist statements written by galleries or agents can often be more marketing pieces than aesthetic statements.) There are two basic forms of a statement: the generalized statement of a body of work done over time and a more particular statement that artists are often asked to prepare about a particular work or series of pieces. It should be no more than 250 words and written in simple, clear, and accessible language. It should be compelling to the reader and address your artistic ideas, influences, any symbolism that you use, and any necessary or interesting information about your technical process.

Language Choices

Language is an important part of communication; the words we speak and write say a lot about us. Virtually every field of endeavour has its own specialized vocabulary—what you would call a "rope," is a "line" or a "halyard" or a "sheet" (depending upon the rope's use) to a sailor. Experts in every vocation develop a specialized vocabulary for their field of study in order to facilitate precise communication, and artists are no different. The language of art criticism and scholarship is far too sophisticated for the artist statement (or résumé or other marketing materials) of most artists seeking advancement in the marketplace, so you must choose your language carefully—every word you choose.

Sometimes it can be appropriate to write about your work or include review quotes about your work in sophisticated language if you are writing about your work for a critical journal, a curator, or an academic environment, for example. But today's art world encompasses people with a broad range of education and experience, so your language must be inclusive and not restrictive. Any idea, no matter how complex, can be presented in plain language. Artist statements are designed to provide contextualization, not a serious intellectual challenge. (And be judicious with your use of adjectives, as they tend to involve judgment; subjectivity rather than objectivity.)

Slide Nights

An excellent tool for artists having difficulty expressing insight into their work is a "slide night" held with peers. Slide nights are great professional development tools for artists, and they are very easy to organize. In this digital age, the hardest part of hosting one may be accessing a slide projector with which to project the slides, which offer brighter, snappier, and more colour-accurate images for viewing. (If you don't have access to a projector, show images from a DVD and view them on TV.)

This is how a slide night works. You invite several artists to a viewing space and ask them to bring five to ten slides of their recent work. Then everyone views and discusses the slides, one artist at a time. When your peers are looking at your slides, you are wise to take notes as they discuss your work, and you do not need to respond unless they ask questions—and don't be defensive. Each person shares his or her observations on your work and you can gain valuable, objective insights from them. Sometimes, brave slide night participants pass around a "what's wrong" or "how can I improve" sheet that allows people to express criticisms in a more comfortable or proactive medium (this way of generating feedback can be anonymous). Your fellow slide night participants can often see trends in your work that you may not see or they will highlight aspects of your work you might not have seen as important. What you learn can be an effective tool for improving your artist statement.

Sample Imagery

The examples of your work that you provide viewers in your portfolio speak loudest about who you are. They are the most important part of your presentation, be they slides, digital images, photographs, videos—whatever is appropriate. Digital imagery is, however, the preferred medium for image submission today. Like your portrait, they should be of professional quality—colour photocopies, snapshots, or ink-jet printed reproductions are not appropriate. If your portfolio contains slides, have a viewer with you when you show your portfolio or ascertain beforehand that the viewer has a light table, slide viewer, or projector. If you have photographs of your work, make sure they are of sufficient size to allow the viewer to see them clearly. You should not have original work in your portfolio.

Choose images to place in your portfolio that are fitting for the purpose of your presentation. Ask yourself why you are choosing each image. What does each image add to the presentation? It is important to have enough samples of your work to speak effectively to your body of work, but not so many that it seems repetitive. Include a complete list of your inventory but be highly selective with your sample imagery.

All the samples of your work in the portfolio must be properly documented, providing all the pertinent information: title, dimensions, materials, and date of completion for two-dimensional work. Performance art documentation, video, film, and multimedia work require additional information such as length of viewing or performance time, technical requirements for exhibiting, and, often, a short descriptive narrative. There are documentation conventions for the various media of the visual arts that are easily obtainable from a variety of sources. The Canada Council for the Arts provides a guideline entitled "The Do's and Don'ts of Submitting Digital Support Material." (*See also Slide Tips Sheet in Appendix C and Digital Image Tips Sheet in Appendix D.*)

Business Cards

Business cards should be part of every portfolio and they should be with you at all times. You never know when you are going to need one—opportunities occur anytime, anywhere. Being a successful small business operator means constant self-promotion. When you are supervising your kids at the playground and you meet another parent with an interest in art, give him/her a business card. When someone beside you at a movie or a play reveals an interest in art, give her/him a business card. When you are shopping in your neighbourhood or meeting a neighbour, give him/her a business card. Distributing your business cards will pay off in the long run and is a very effective part of the artist's marketing mix. It builds awareness of your artistic practice and is very cost effective—business cards today are inexpensive, even if they carry an image. (And whenever you give out a card, try to capture the recipient's contact information so you can add it to the appropriate section of your mailing list and, if you want, follow up on the meeting.)

Brochures

The cost of printing—especially digital printing—has dropped considerably in recent years. It is now affordable to print full colour brochures. As with business cards, brochures can be effective marketing tools when placed in the hands of people with whom a relationship has been established—especially when partnered with cover letters. They can be an enhancement to communication with individuals, but they are too commercial to use when seeking an interview with a gallery or applying for inclusion in an exhibition. They can be useful when replying to expressions of interest growing from an exhibition, website, or word-of-mouth advertising. Brochures say much more than a business card, but say far, far less than in a portfolio presentation.

Good brochures must not simply repeat information of your other marketing materials—you can repeat points, but in new language. Your brochures should engage the readers and direct them to your website, studio, email address, and/or phone number for more in-depth information. Use images in the brochure that do not appear elsewhere in your materials. Keep everything fresh; have a new way of presenting your information in every marketing tool and, as with everything, keep it clean and crisp. Use language that is simple and straightforward. Have it professionally designed if you are not strong in commercial graphic design, use professional-quality images and ensure the writing is compelling, grammatically correct, and free of spelling errors.

Testimonials are a highly convincing component of brochures (and other promotional tools). Get permission to quote those who speak or write positively about your work in your brochures and other marketing materials. Have different testimonials for your brochure and your website so that there is no repetition. Use your strongest testimonials on the brochure because they are very effective text for consumers—especially if the speaker quoted is well known or a recognized authority (by name or title).

***An important note*:** Brochures have a very commercial connotation. Artists uncomfortable about appearing too focused on the marketplace may want to avoid the brochure altogether, but for those artists comfortable with self-promotion, the brochure becomes an "extended" business card.

Postcards

Perhaps the most popular form of print communication for visual artists is the postcard. It has been used as an art form as an extension of mail art, but it is a format that is very popular with artists for advertising. Full-colour postcards are easy to produce today; they can be an inexpensive and visually striking way to invite or inform potential buyers. Google "cheap postcards" to search for local Canadian postcard-printing businesses such as Club Card (clubcard.ca), Copythis (copythis.ca), and Vertical Thinking (verticalthinking.ca).

These sites make using their services very easy. You can upload files, order, and pay online, and your postcards can be delivered. The more you print, the cheaper per postcard. Postcards can serve as large business cards—providing more information than a normal business card, but less information and a less commercial impression than a brochure.

The key is successful design. Your postcard has to stand out; it has to make viewers want to read more about what they see at first glance. Although many software programs and websites have design templates that you can use to easily create a decent design, they often require that you use the host's printing services and that can be considerably more expensive than competitive printers. Get professional design services if you cannot do it yourself then prepare the file for printing yourself.

Sales Tags

Pay attention to this concept. The value of sales tags is significant and few artists understand their value. Sales tags are price tags with biographical information on them—tiny short biographies that include (safe) contact information such as your blog or website address if you have one.

Sales tags are inappropriate for smaller or commercial products that some artists make, but there should be a sales tag on every piece of real artistic work that you sell. When you have a show or are part of a group exhibition, sales tags are inappropriate. However, when work sells from an exhibition, the gallery should separately provide your biography and conservation information to the buyer.

It is well known that many buyers of art become repeat buyers of the same artist. Effective art marketers understand that buyers often view their purchase of an artwork as an investment in the artist. As such, they want to know more about the person in whom they have invested. They value a relationship with the artist that enhances their purchase. Buyers, after all, value the responses of their guests to their artwork. And when a buyer's guest says, "I love your new painting," he or she enjoy being able to respond to the compliment with information about the artist. Even more valuable for the buyer is a response that reveals personal stories of contact with the artist.

When a gallery sells your work or a work is sold from an exhibition, you are often not there to meet the buyer. The sales tag that you provide the vendor to accompany sales, therefore, is very important. It is a step toward the establishment of a relationship. If your sales tag invites the buyer to email you or visit your website, you have the opportunity to develop the relationship further. Most importantly, the contact can allow you to add the buyer's name to your mailing list. (Artists with representation will have this service provided by their gallery but will not often want the artist to communicate directly with the buyer.)

Public Speaking Skills

Your portfolio is usually presented to viewers in person. The ability to speak effectively to one person or a group can give an artist a very powerful marketing advantage because it allows you to make several relationships at once. If you can comfortably speak to groups about your work, you can do wonders to further public awareness of your practice, and this can mean that you can likely teach as well. Many community colleges offer courses on public speaking and they include instruction on the development of speeches. Teachers of public speaking courses are often available as coaches to help you perfect a presentation that can be made over and over again to different groups. Also, you can use the slide-night format (described earlier in this chapter) to practice publicly speaking with other artists, seeking to develop a compelling oral presentation.

Artists who can make interesting oral presentations about being an artist, the creative process, or about their own work, can find many opportunities to deliver their message and forge new relationships. Besides docent work in galleries, many of your local organizations such as colleges, libraries, arts councils, community centres, church groups, youth groups and seniors groups, value guests who deliver interesting presentations. If they are good speakers, and if they develop an interesting presentation (or more than one), each appearance can create opportunities. And when you do make public presentations, remember to distribute your business card or brochure—something that includes your contact information.

NINE

Promotion

"In all of the world so far, I'm the greatest, greatest star!"

—Bob Merrill, lyricist for Funny Girl
(From the song, "The Greatest Star")

"Promotion is something you do all the time throughout your career. Publicity is something you undertake infrequently; publicity is media-focused and time-specific." *— C. T.*

Introduction

As self-employed businesspersons, artists must be involved with self-promotion all the time and for the length of their career. Whereas publicity is a form of promotion that is infrequent, time-specific, and focused on the media, self-promotion is a key developmental strategy that is ongoing. Self-promotion involves a standardized approach to informing the public (customer) about you and your product(s). Good promotional work persuades the customer to take an interest in you and your product(s) or service(s). It is undertaken to influence your customers; it assists you in establishing a relationship with your marketplace.

Artists with thriving businesses are often those who make themselves and/or their work visible any way (and every way) they can. They are experts at self-promotion and they direct their promotional efforts to the right people and the right market(s).

Sometimes self-promotion is almost unnecessary when the artist is a creative genius. The tiny percentage of visual artists with a genius vision can increase if they simply stay focused on creation—others will do their promotional work for them (curators, their galleries, and the media). Still, even artists with tremendous talent can improve their success if they are effective self-promoters. People have to know about you in order to want your work—awareness precedes desire, and promotion is about building awareness, or building a reputation.

One's reputation as a citizen, as a member of a class or a group, is the equivalent of corporate branding. To some extent, we can control or manage our reputation; in some ways we cannot. As small businesses, artists want to involve themselves with promotional methods that allow them to retain some control. These methods include creating name recognition, advertising, "placement," third-party promotions (including endorsements), salons, and art rentals. (One has little-to-no control over word-of-mouth advertising, reviews, and sometimes, the outcomes of publicity initiatives.)

All contemporary artists must undertake promotion in earnest in order to maximize income from their creative practice.

Name Recognition

Visual artists want their work to be seen; many want their work to sell. Regardless of your objective, promotion is designed to make your name known as widely as possible—at least in the right circles. You want your name to come to mind when curators plan their exhibitions, when the people on your mailing list want to buy some art or art services, or when local organizations want to offer art courses, in the same way that Walmart wants their name to come to mind when you want to buy something. What you and Walmart want, is name recognition. All the money that Walmart puts into marketing and all the effort they put into their promotions are designed simply to have you know and remember one word: Walmart. Your promotional effort is about doing the same thing. Your name is the baseline message of all promotion that you do (including all your professional conversations, emails, the greeting on your answering machine, and your stationery, business cards, invitations, and media releases).

The baseline message is the one short message that you want to leave in people's minds. It could be one of the following or a short combination of them:

- John Doe
- John Doe, Artist
- John Doe, Master Printmaker (your medium)
- John Doe, MFA (your degree)
- John Doe, Master Impressionist (your style or marketing niche)
- John Doe, Excellence in Interior Decoration (a sales-oriented qualifier)
- JohnDoe.ca (your website or blog address)

Having a standard baseline message as part of all your communications and at the forefront of all you do in the way of promotion and publicity helps to create your name (brand) recognition.

Artists at the beginning of their careers should show their work in every *appropriate* setting possible—inventory that sits in their studios does nothing for them. They need to get their work into places where potential buyers assemble—places where people with disposable income and good taste gather, such as corporate offices, medical offices, boardrooms, banks, spas, country clubs, golf clubs, and yacht clubs.

Example: Suzanne

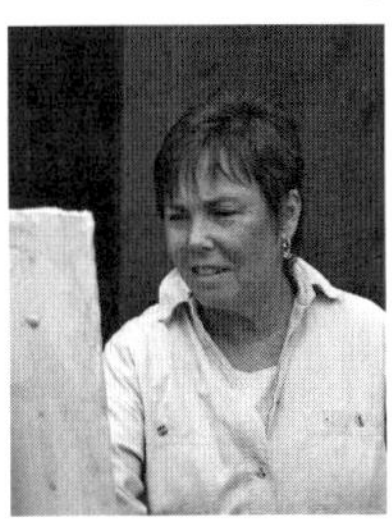

Suzanne is an artist who prefers to work in acrylics. Her "cash cow," however, is her line of monoprints. She began producing monoprints because the high-earning professionals to whom she sells do not understand the printmaking world and terminology. She likes monoprints because they are each unique "originals," but are made in the semi mass-production method of monoprinting. She can produce a series of works that have obvious similarities yet each one is also unique. She produces several series of monoprints each year.

Suzanne's target buyers are working professionals such as doctors, lawyers, accountants, stockbrokers, and realtors. She routinely visits corporate offices and leaves immediately if they have original art on their walls. But if they have cheap or tasteless prints or posters on their walls, she asks the receptionist for the name of the office manager or partner in charge of office management or marketing, and then she next sends the contact a proposal package that has one resonating statement and an offer: Statement: "Bad art earns bad customers," she tells them. "Bad art says to your clients and employees that you don't care about their environment and that you have no taste." Offer: "Rent my *original* art—you don't even have to buy it—and I'll change it every six months or every year."

Her approach is very successful. When she meets with the corporate client, she offers them her paintings (to buy or rent) or monoprints (that are priced only for sales). Her prices are both reasonable and negotiable.

Suzanne provides information about herself and her work to the staff of the whole firm in each location where she places her art. Many individuals of the firms have since become buyers of her work. "I feel that some of the firms who have my work on their walls, think of me as a kind of artist in residence," she says. "They invite me to some events and parties and kind of show me off as their proud little bauble."

Exposure

Self-promotion is about exposure. The object, as with effective advertising, is to have people of the right demographics see your name and/or work as often as possible. To that end, many artists place their work in locations such as restaurants, coffee shops, hair salons, clothing boutiques, bookstores, hotels, bed and breakfasts, and furniture showrooms. These alternate places almost never produce a sale, but viewers can be exposed to your baseline message if you are selective about where you install your work. And if you do use such venues (and this can be a vital vehicle for sales in small towns and vacation townships), display your work in a way that emulates a gallery experience—well lit and protected from becoming damaged. Work that is poorly displayed will have viewers associating your name with work that is not valued or respected. Finally, if you can place your work in a venue where a staff member knows you and will point your work out to customers, so much the better.

Artists can also improve the exposure of their name by:

1. Doing volunteer work for not-for-profit visual art organizations and other charities.
2. Donating their services to make public art.
3. Teaching (for art clubs, community centres, colleges, seniors homes, churches, and community groups).
4. Doing demonstrations at art fairs and/or in art supply stores.
5. Mastering the art of publicity.
6. Creating qualitative product(s) for specialized niche markets.
7. Placing works in charity auctions for visual art organizations (*see chapter five*).

Publicity

Media publicity is by far the promotional tool having the highest impact, but getting it is a significant challenge. And if you are successful at attracting the attention of the media, it happens rarely, so you must save your effort for the right time. The next chapter is concerned with publicity, but below are other ways to advance your career.

Advertising

Media advertising is largely irrelevant to individual artists. Your gallery may undertake some advertising on your behalf, but it is your self-promotion materials (business card, website, or brochure) that are your primary advertising tools.

One form of advertising that is extremely valuable for visual artists is direct marketing. Direct marketing (by mail, email, or phone) is the most important and cost-effective form of advertising available to the artist/small businessperson.

Advertising does become relevant when artists act cooperatively. Christmas craft fairs or other seasonal markets and collective open studio events can often afford to use media advertising as part of their marketing strategy—sharing the advertising costs amongst the participants. These types of events can often bargain with media (especially if they are non-profit organizations) to get community or sponsorship rates. When collectives advertise, however, it is important to know that advertising once is a useless exercise. Advertising works as a "multiple-hit" strategy—each advertisement reinforces the message of others in the same campaign over time and/or in other media outlets; it's not a one-time, one-place "shot."

When advertising is undertaken, work with a professional copywriter or graphic artist to create advertisements that work. Creating effective ads is an art and a science. As a creative person, you can create unique and powerful advertising, but creating beautiful ads is not the goal. Ads that motivate people to do what you want is your objective. Ads that inspire attendance at your event are the only kind of ads you want to produce.

Third-Party Promotion

An obvious example of a third-party promotion is the work done by a gallery to promote an exhibition of your work. Published or otherwise circulated on your behalf, third-party promotions are powerful because they have the appearance of objectivity. They are usually the result of collaboration between the artist and the gallery owner and are less than objective.

Artists who place wholesale or consignment products in a retail outlet may benefit from sales promotions by the retailer. If you have product in such a setting, your product likely has competition in the outlet. If your work is in a retail outlet, you may need to ask if it is featured in displays, is at eye level and well lit, and if it is in the retailer's advertising. You can make your product stand out in a retail outlet by having display material close at hand—this is a site-specific form of promotion.

Besides the right vendor for your commercial art products, the right place in the vendor's outlet has an impact on your sales. Well-known brands fight for eye-level placement in supermarket shelves. Good places in retail outlets have high visibility, good traffic flow, and a high volume of sales. The right outlet has a serious marketing budget, a customer base interested in your type of artistic product, a good sales team and customer service, fair pricing, and prompt payment to you when your work sells. At a crafts fair or in a market, being stationed near the entrance is better than being at the back—so is being near the food or a lounge.

Salons

A salon is an effective name to use for a reception in your studio, in your home, or on the premises of a third party. A salon in your home is very personal and can further your relationship with your best customers or a group of potential customers. Salons are invitation-only events and feature work that is for sale, but almost parenthetically—the focus is on building the relationship with attendees (past good clients, potential clients) not on the sales that may occur. Artists with a strong sales history and many clients can advance relationships well by hosting a salon.

Third-party salons take place in the residence or office of a good client and often with the purpose of the host building new relationships with friends and colleagues. The host invites clients, friends, and business associates to the salon, and the artist invites a few key buyers whom she or he knows will mix well with the host and who will provide good words about the artist and the art. Buyers often enjoy hosting this kind of event, as it shows them as patrons of the arts, philanthropic, and community minded. (Consider the words of Suzanne [in the previous example] and her relationship with her host.) The artist sometimes gives the host an artwork and collects from the host the contact information of all who attended the event for his or her mailing list. Several artists who have used this model suggest that the number of guests be limited and that the invitations speak to the "special nature" of the event (engraved invitations are good!). Invitations should say in every way that this is a special event, not just another sale or opening.

Example: Brie

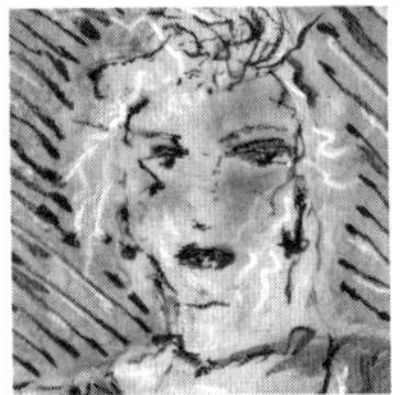

Brie has a studio in her home. She is stay-at-home mom to three kids. She celebrates motherhood in her artwork that features designs drawn from the home—particularly the kitchen, her children, and food. Her paintings sell well, so she started making limited-edition prints of some of her work. She has not had the time to do the marketing needed to sell her work, but one day she had a salon in the foyer of an accounting firm. Several of the accountants in the firm wanted to keep the images around when the show was over; they proposed renting the pieces so that they could be changed from time to time. Brie set a rate of $15 per piece per month, and they rented twenty prints. Brie changes the prints every year. This deal makes her $300 per month and it has lasted over three years so far. Her total contract benefit to date is $12,600. (Why didn't the accountants buy the pieces? They like the tax credits of leasing programs; the firm leases all they can.)

Word-of-Mouth Advertising

Word-of-mouth advertising is very relevant to the artist/small businessperson. It is something you can influence, but not control. Good word of mouth can yield great testimonials, and there is no better copy for marketing than a good testimonial, especially if it comes from a knowledgeable, respected, or well-known source. The more customers you have, the better they are treated; the more they like your product, the more good word-of-mouth advertising you are going to get. But use pigments that fade too quickly in the light, deliver product late or of poor quality, or produce product of varying quality and word-of-mouth advertising will be soon working against you. Word of mouth is a two-way street.

Reviews

A review is an excellent outcome of a promotional or publicity initiative. Reviews are the result of (self) promotion and improve name recognition, but getting an exhibition is hard work and getting reviewed is even harder. Getting reviewed by a credible art critic is accomplished by only a small percentage of artists. Artists are rarely reviewed as a result of their initiative; they are usually reviewed as a result of their gallery's efforts or because of their already established reputation. In smaller towns, artists may have easier access to a review that is often written by a journalist; these reviews are usually soft news—community stories in the vein of "what's going on" information. Getting reviewed requires drive, talent, patience, skill, and a dedicated focus to your work, for many years.

TEN

Publicity

"Surely nothing has to listen to so many stupid remarks as a painting in a museum."
—*Edmond & Jules de Goncourt*

"Publicity happens when you stand out; it does not make you stand out."
—*C. T.*

What Is Publicity?

Publicity is a form of promotion that focuses on a specific event (e.g., an exhibition, sale, commission, or award ceremony) and is media focused. Good publicity is planned and has a message. For visual artists, that message usually is: "Know who I am" or "Come to my show or sale (and buy my work)." Publicity campaigns are often aimed at daily newspapers, television, or radio; although, social networking websites such as Facebook, MySpace, or YouTube are increasingly influential publicity vehicles for artists.

Media publicity is valuable not only because it is free exposure, but also because it is nearly always favourable (unlike a review or critique). Media exposure gives artists visibility that may suddenly and dramatically affect their careers. Publicity happens when artists stand out; it does not make artists stand out. Publicity is earned. Artists must undertake a (modest-to-significant) media campaign, or strategy, to obtain exposure, and which can range in scale and sophistication.

When you are successful in generating broadcast or print media interest in you or your (collective or individual) work, it is free advertising, with the added value of the objective voice of the journalist—an apparent endorsement. When you get media coverage, readers and/or viewers see your publicity as approval of your work and career.

Planning a Publicity Campaign

Achieving a broadcast interview, print feature article, or media sponsorship requires the following strategic elements:

1. Understanding media relevance: Is your story relevant to the media? Are you approaching relevant media? Is there a right time for your campaign?
2. Having and using excellent campaign tools: a media release or public service announcement (PSA); sample visuals and/or audio clips; written stories and biographies.
3. Implementing a media-relations strategy: planning how to approach the media and how to respond to them; obtaining and following up with the right contacts.
4. Developing a very strong lead: a hook, pitch, or gimmick.
5. Delivering your objective: your campaign's goal is to get people to

the show, sale, or award ceremony; you must have a "call to action."

6. Being prepared for the delivery event and for any and all consequences of your campaign: inventory is ready, and informational materials (e.g., business cards, samples, biography, résumé, and illustrations) are provided to journalists who respond to your media release; you have rehearsed your story and can tell it well, and will be available for any and all media requests.

Urban Media

Arts editors, the media gatekeepers, are busy people. They cover the topics of food, fashion, literature, the performing arts, fairs, festivals, film, museums and history, and the fine arts—all in a small section of newspapers and in hiccups of broadcast media (except the CBC, and particularly, Radio Canada). It is, therefore, extremely hard for the visual artist to get publicity in major media in most large Canadian cities—if there is time and space available in arts media coverage, it is mostly given to the performing arts and film.

The arts editor in print media or the show producer in broadcast media decides which journalists will cover what story—they may take an interest in you, but their take on your story may end up being presented in the context of a community feature, a home decorating story, or part of a feature on gardening, health, ethnicity, or many artists. If your work has an obvious niche or target market (e.g., art about sports, religion, or animals), the appropriate media, departments, and journalists must be the focus of your campaign.

Community Media

The arts media situation changes in smaller community-centered media outlets, such as small-town or neighbourhood newspapers, community-access television, ethnic or religious media, and special-interest or corporate communications.

Community media outlets are accessible to the individual artist who is a member of that community directly or through family, friends, or association. Many of us belong to many communities—be they religious, professional, linguistic, geographic, or recreational. You can readily gain access to these media outlets if your story is somehow relevant to their specialized audience. If you are the most accomplished artist or even the only artist in a small community, your local media are likely to be responsive to you. Your location, lifestyle, or passions can provide the "hook" you need for interest of the community media.

In some cases, you may be searching for a market for your products, in other cases you might be searching for a product for a market to which you belong. If you love to draw or paint marine scenes, for example, yacht club newsletters may be a good publicity vehicle if you can earn the interest of club administrators and get access to their newsletter or membership list. Otherwise, if you know a member of the club who can successfully advocate for you, you may be able to show the work at the club. But if you belong to a yacht club, developing a product for the club may be an ideal opportunity for you to market to club members.

If you are not a member of a yacht club, you may belong to a church, alumni society, professional organization, linguistic or cultural group, golf club, academic community, or sports team. These are all examples of communities that often have newsletters, websites, gatherings, conventions, and membership lists that make them ideal niche markets for the entrepreneurial artist.

Arts Media

Publications with an arts mandate are obvious targets for the mailing lists and publicity campaigns of visual artists, but competition for inclusion can be intense. Access to these outlets usually requires that you achieve a significant career milestone, are part of something truly unique or topical, are well publicized, or are championed by a respected gallery or curator.

Arts-focused broadcasts can be slightly more accessible because they are often concerned with public accessibility. They will be interested in unique or popular events and often feature interesting stories on individual artists. Accessing arts broadcasts is best achieved by means of an effective publicity campaign, but even a cold call can lead to success for a story with a good aural hook.

An informed audience reads arts media. Exposure to an arts-focused outlet can have a significant impact on an artist's career—curators and gallery owners read arts publications—yet they are not vital to the publicity campaigns of artists focusing on sales. General media outlets and appropriate media for niche or target marketing are far more relevant for sales and name recognition within the general population.

The Individual vs. the Collective Campaign

Individual artists will be most often involved with publicity in partnership with their gallery when they are having an exhibition. Still, as your career grows, you will meet media representatives that you should always add to your mailing list. Over time and with work, you will build up your list. Be careful to note those journalists with whom you actually develop a relationship—these people merit special treatment of your own invention, keeping them aware without being too communicative. When you have your own annotated media list but are acting as part of a collective, the collective will appreciate having you be their contact person for those media reps with whom you have rapport.

Publicity in the visual arts is rarely about the individual artists unless they have achieved a career milestone or created a genius body of work. Visual artists can be more successful with the media when they work as a collective. Initiatives such as neighbourhood open studios are very popular in Vancouver, for example: Artists in our Midst (artistsinourmidst.com), Eastside Culture Crawl (eastsideculturecrawl.com), Swarm (an initiative of the Pacific Association of Artist Run Centres—paarc.ca [click on "Swarm"]), and The Circle Craft Christmas Market (circlecraft.net).

When you act as a collective, your size of your organization is the hook to which the media responds. When Vancouver artists came together to undertake the Artists in our Midst or Eastside Culture Crawl, for example, the media responded because of the number of artists involved and because of the size of the expected audience. Each year, these events enjoy respectable coverage in local media (like a three-page spread in Vancouver's largest daily in 2007) because they:

1. Create dynamic, exciting visual material for cameras and microphones.
2. Involve a large number of artists and a large number of visitors.

3. Are free for attendees.
4. Are stimulating, educational, and of varied experience.
5. Are appropriate for people of every age.
6. Afford visitors a unique shopping opportunity.

There are a few critical things to consider when working as a collective. For example, choosing representative images and the right spokespersons. Not everyone can be featured in the publicity campaign. A jury, a guest curator, or (even better) a marketing expert can help select campaign imagery. The artists with the most visually compelling or provocative work or an incredible story should be featured in the publicity materials. Collectives can distribute duties among members so that many artists share in campaign responsibility, each doing what he or she does best.

The Circle Craft Collective in Vancouver has an annual Christmas show. Each year, an invited guest jury selects the best artist's booth in the show. The selected artist receives an award and her or his work is featured in all the publicity materials of the following year's event.

Example: Artropolis

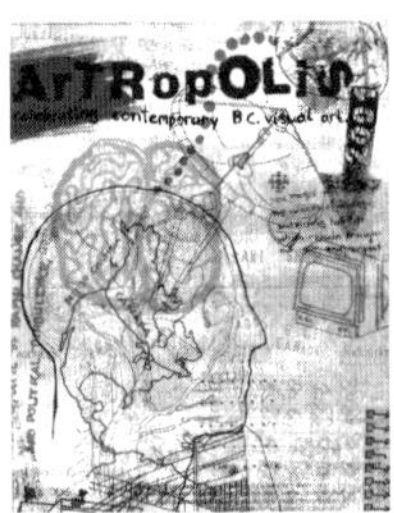

No better example of collective action exists than Vancouver's Artropolis exhibitions that were held in Vancouver in 1987, 1990, 1993, 1997, 2001, and 2003. The organization's purpose was to feature the works of contemporary British Columbia artists in non-traditional exhibition spaces. Its impetus came from the success of the October Show (1983) and Warehouse Show (1984). These predecessors to Artropolis began as "salons des réfusés," in reaction to the Vancouver Art Gallery's plans for the show Art and Artists: 1931 to 1983, celebrating the gallery's re-opening in new facilities. Art and Artists was considered too exclusive by members of the Vancouver art community and so, in response, the October Show was conceived and organized collaboratively and featured over 120 artists. In the decades that followed, the Artropolis shows were extremely popular with the media and the public. Media coverage focused on a fortunate few each year, but up to 5,000 people per week saw the work of hundreds of a great number of contemporary BC artists.

Your Mailing List: Media Listings

One section of a mailing list should be for journalists and you should have codes to enable you to target sub-groups on your list. If you are making product that is relevant to a particular niche market (e.g., designers, gardeners, or a particular sport) your media list should include relevant journalists or editors, and be coded and noted as such. If you have a diverse product line, you may have different media contacts for different products. Coding enables you to keep everything in order. You can have codes for many characteristics of each media contact on your list. Media categories include:

Print:

1. Newspapers: national or local dailies, weeklies, regional publications, and ethnic or other special interest.
2. Magazines: monthly, quarterly, annual, and ethnic or other special interest.
3. Newsletters: corporate and public.

Broadcast:

1. Television: local, provincial, national, and ethnic or special interest.
2. Radio: local, national, ethnic or other special interest, and Sirius Satellite.
3. Web: podcasts and social media (such as Facebook, MySpace, etc.).

You must choose the right editors and journalists for print media, the right stations and programs in broadcast media, and the right newsletter or website contact for your campaign. Do your research: know your objectives and identify the right media targets. List by journalist, not media; there may be several relevant journalists in one media outlet (e.g., CBC Radio or The Globe and Mail). Different journalists cover listings, for example, than those who write feature stories; home-décor journalists may be relevant for your media list. Make note of the preferences of each journalist when you can: his or her field of expertise, any weaknesses (I have met a visual arts critic who was colour blind), and any other notes you can help you develop your relationship with media personalities.

Emerging or beginning artists and artists living in smaller communities may wisely include buyers, post-secondary art instructors, foundations, bureaucrats, prominent citizens, or other categories of people as contacts on their publicity lists as well as media names. Choose whatever is right for you, your situation, your story, and your level. Building a good list takes time and research, but in major urban centres, there are arts collectives, galleries, and artists with lists they will sell or lend to you. (*See chapter six for the importance of maintaining a good mailing list.*)

Example: Mary-J

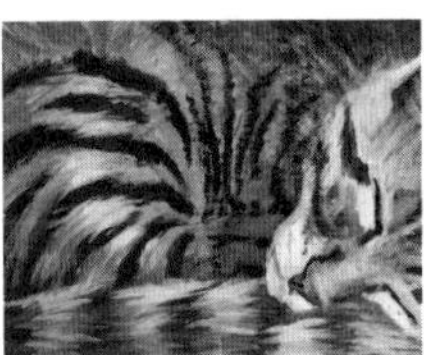

Mary-J creates artwork with integrity that is the focus of her career. She codes the names of people on her media list who are relevant to her career (reviewers, curators, peers, frequent or important buyers, etc.) and she directs her career-focused media campaigns to these people. But she also makes money doing pet portraits under a *nom de plume*. For this area of her career, she has pet-relevant codes on her media list for lifestyle journalists, veterinarians, and pet stores so that her publicity campaigns can be career or pet-relevant campaigns. Mary-J has very effective publicity materials for her campaign aimed at veterinarians and pet storeowners. She pays a commission on each portrait to the SPCA; this practice has her enjoying the active support of the vet and store employees who display her pet portrait advertising materials prominently in their offices and stores.

Is There a Right Time for Your Campaign?

When milestone events (like an award, a large, important, and/or international commission, a retrospective exhibition, or a public art installation) happen to an artist, this is likely the only time the media will take an interest in the individual for a feature story. Otherwise, a media campaign, if focused on an exhibition or sale, will often only result in a listing in a community events calendar. If you have a particularly striking image or a media reputation, however, your work may be used to illustrate the calendar or event-listing section.

Milestones can be the ignition for a campaign, but they are not the whole story—the artist's entire career is the story. The right time to approach the media, however, may not be when such an event occurs. For example, Brent got a large Canada Council grant to do site-specific work in abandoned prairie homesteads. The photographic documentation of his site-specific installations became exhibition material for his galleries in Toronto and Vancouver. In the same space of time, he was selected to be part of a show in a well-known American showcase exhibition of contemporary art. Fortunately for Brent, about two months before the first exhibition of his work in a Vancouver gallery, the town council in control of one of the homestead's Brent had used, voted in favour to preserve the cabin. The municipality cited Brent's work as one reason the council had finally taken action.

Just prior to the opening of his first show on the cabins, he issued a media release to BC media contacts with the headline, "Artist Saves Historic Site." His release received a lot of interest and Brent enjoyed a tremendous response to his campaign. He did the same thing in Toronto. All his accomplishments made for a rich and potent campaign—a good story with an interesting delivery (his exhibition). He timed his campaign on his show/sale; he did not issue a release when he got his grant or completed his installations. He focused on the exhibition because it produced sales and because he knew the hook grew with each component—grant, historical theme, saving a cabin, and the exhibition. His campaign furthered public awareness of his name and served as a personal introduction to many media journalists whose relationships, over time, may prove valuable.

Besides being at the right time in terms of your career, there are better times than others in the calendar year to approach the media. If you are part of a group of artists planning a collective exhibition, choose an appropriate time in the calendar year if you can. In large cities, September and October are a busy months for the arts; so is pre-Christmas time. Choosing to have a group exhibition during these times increases your competition for media attention, but if your collective event is sales focused, even though it is a time with a lot of competition, you may want to plan your event to coincide with the Christmas spending season. Summertime is often a time when the media is more accessible; this season can be a slow news time and a good sales time if there are tourists for your collective to access.

What Is a Media Campaign?

The central tool of any media campaign is the press, or media, release that may or may not be supported by other materials. The message is clear and simple in a release, and leads to a "delivery." With your research done, you know who are the important media targets and you know their lead-time (some periodicals have deadlines three months prior to publication). Your media release, all support materials, your spokesperson (if you have one), and selective and representative imagery all have to be in place two weeks ahead of the earliest deadline.

Don't issue your release to everyone at once. If you are targeting a magazine with a three-month deadline, issue your release only to them. As the deadlines of your target media approach, send your release to them, doing the mass release to everyone at least two-to-three weeks ahead of your event. There must be enough time for you to circulate it, allow for a "digestion time," and then call the most important targets on your list to follow up.

Start with the Story

There is no publicity campaign without a story. And at its core must be sufficient valuable information for the general public in order to justify media interest. As has been said, your story must be relevant to the media and, it should have a great "hook," for example: "Artist X has just been awarded a grant to enable a residency deep inside the Arctic Circle," or, "Artist X has just been awarded a grant to enable a residency deep inside the Arctic Circle that will allow her to revisit the sites where her father painted watercolours in 1942." The first example is a good story, if aimed at arts journalists, because of the Arctic Circle hook. However, the second example is better—there are two hooks: the Arctic and the inter-generational story. The trick is to have an irresistible story that has great visual. The media love stories about people. The media objective of most visual artists is not a hard news story (except in rare cases about theft, career achievement, copyrights, or taxation, for example). Instead, your story is likely to be a soft news story—one that is written by a journalist who is a generalist or a critic (but writing in a non-critical capacity).

Brent, mentioned earlier, had a great story. It started with getting a grant, which led to a very interesting story about using abandon heritage homes as sets for works staged for documentation, and then the bonus—one town moving to save the cabin, partly as a result of Brent's bringing "outside" attention to a community asset suffering neglect. And then there was his exhibition that provided excellent visuals for the print journalists and, at the opening, great sound bytes for broadcast media.

The Media Release

Writing an effective media release is an art. It is written in a persuasive style; its success is measured by its effect. (*See Chapter Eleven and Appendix E.*)

The first reader of a media release is often a research assistant in large media outlets, or an editor or journalist in other cases. Whoever reads your release is often reading scores of them. The job of your release is to stand out from others: to grab the (often cynical) reader's interest and compel him or her to action on your behalf. The larger the media outlet you are targeting, the more skilled will be the release reader who selects the stories or listings to pursue. There are four important components of a media release: identity, the headline, the body, and the delivery.

1. Identity: The top of the media release must first identify the sender: the collective producer of the event or the individual artist (perhaps in the form of a letterhead). (Media releases composed by the artists themselves are weak compared to all others; self-promotion suggests a lack of interest by others in the community. It is better to have a third party be the sender of your media release.) Also identify the date of the release, and the name, phone numbers, and email of contact personnel, and in large print, the words "Media Release"; these shall be the next things that the viewer sees.
2. The headline: The headline must be compelling. Its sole purpose is to immediately engage the reader, motivating him or her to read the release. The headline (and the first sentence of the body) should hit hard with the hook or pitch line.
3. The body: Now that you've grabbed the reader with the headline, the first paragraph has to convince the media person that she or he was wise to keep reading. It should elaborate on the headline and develop further interest in your subject.

   For most visual artists, the body of a media release will focus on an exhibition or sale; standard event media releases address the basic information regarding who, what, when, where, why, and how. An extremely effective part of the body can be a testimonial—particularly if the quotation comes from a well-known and/or respected person. Add copy as long as you continue to build interest that leads to your delivery. Do not exceed one page.

4. The delivery: The delivery answers the question, what is the reader to do? The last paragraph provides this direction. Your reader is told when, where, and how to see the show, written in a succinct manner. You can repeat information here or provide it for the first time, but this is the information readers are to be left with—this and the hook.

Media Release Writing Tips

The five W's in point form: (be as brief as possible) write the particulars of who, what, where, when, why (i.e. values), and how (i.e. transportation, parking, handicap access, how to get more information, or how to get tickets). Note any other interesting and relevant points, and then rank all your essential points in order of interest.

Turn your points into text, writing like a news reporter—make it easy for journalists by providing them with the appropriate information for their stories; never exceed one page, but you can attach or include a separate written "story" from which they can excerpt text and any quotes.

Use simple clear language: avoid "artspeak" and language that may feel like jargon to the reader; be upbeat but do not exaggerate.

Read and re-read your release: edit judiciously, read it aloud, and have colleagues read and edit it as well.

Digital Media Releases

Peter has a long and successful history with the media. His father was an editor in a large daily newspaper in Vancouver. His media releases are PDF files and he comfortably violates the "one page only" commandment. His media release remains complete on one page, but it has additional pages containing support materials. The front page, the release itself, has a link to his blog where interested parties can download still or moving images and sound bytes as support materials for his release. It is fast, inexpensive, flashy, efficient, and rich with information, and is impressive as a way to open media doors. His recipients can make their decision about his pitch by reading the first page and if they get hooked, all the support material is right there for them. Peter is very successful at getting the media to feature his projects in a competitive urban market.

Collectives will appreciate the digital model Peter uses because the release itself is one page, but there can be support materials provided that disburse focus over numerous participants. Also, listing all the participants' websites is an excellent appendix for a collective media release, as can be the provision of an easily accessible pictorial resource for journalists (hosted on a website).

The PSA

The public service announcement (PSA) is a particular form of media release. It can be aimed at broadcast journalists (or departments) and the full text that is provided can be usually read in a finite number of seconds— often ten to thirty. PSAs can be text on paper, a short video or film on CD or DVD, and/or a tape recording (with or without 2-D visual materials). It is a quick, catchy summary of the information contained in the media release of the campaign of which it is a part *(see Appendix F)*. Like the media release, it is sent to appropriate journalists in appropriate media. Many media outlets have one contact address for PSAs and other ones for media releases. (Always indicate the length of time of your PSA—or times, if your PSA is presented in two forms.)

Audio Visual Support: Samples & Examples

Part of every good media campaign is the support material you can provide to journalists whose interest you attract through your media release. If a journalist contacts you, you should immediately make the journalist feel that she or he has made the right decision in getting back to you—the best way to reward a responding journalist is to have dynamic support materials ready, such as an effective spokesperson and good illustrative materials. An effective spokesperson is someone who is an excellent speaker—captivating but efficient in his or her responses; an extrovert who is articulate, knowledgeable, charismatic, media savvy, and "programmed" to speak for the collective (and not him or herself). Good illustrative materials are still images, video clips, or access to easy taping opportunities; sound bytes from participants or principals involved; background materials such as biographies and photos of principals; and a list of participants' (or selected participants') websites, phone numbers, and emails.

For many rural media outlets, community media publications, and newsletters, it can be valuable for artists to have their story written out. Sometimes, it will be published as it is written if it is not too long, is well written, and of interest—especially if there is a good still image to support it. Do not exaggerate or enhance anything; be honest, positive, confident, and interesting. A good article will be an extended version of the media release, building to the same delivery, but with more information—all compelling, and none redundant. Also, brief (!) written biographies of principals can be valuable support materials.

Hooks / Gimmicks

Anything is fair in pursuit of publicity—but always be 100% truthful. When a story is about one artist, it is usually about a single achievement by the artist—that is the story's hook, whether it be a show, an award, a commission.

Example: Victoria

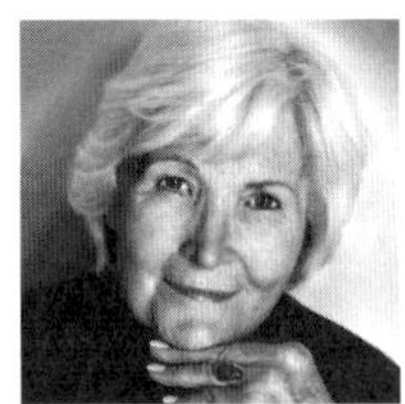

Victoria was achieving modest commercial success when she was diagnosed with cancer. She learned about visualization during her treatment, and that led to a desire to paint what she was visualizing during her therapy for her friends and therapist to see. When she showed her caregivers what she was doing, they arranged for her to show her work in the treatment centre. That in turn led to media exposure; a health journalist approached Victoria about using her work to illustrate a story she was writing about breast cancer. That led to the hospital publishing one of her posters to sell as a fundraiser at their events, through their mailing list and the hospital gift shop. (Victoria gets a commission on each poster sale.)

Example: Damian

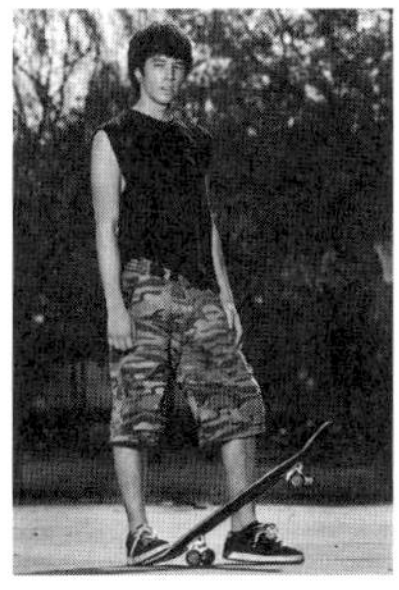

Damian is an artist who creates rough, edgy art. He knew the simple nature of his artwork had him viewed as outside the mainstream and unlikely to be considered seriously by critics, buyers, and the media. Consequently, he proposed an exhibition of "outsider art" to a local community centre and they accepted it. He showed the selection committee the works he wanted to include in the show and many were from outside Canada, but every artist was willing to pay for the costs of sending their work to Damian.

The show was a hit—particularly with entertainment journalists responsible for reporting "what's on." A whole genre of art—outsider art—was introduced to a wide audience in both print and broadcast media. Damian selected a broad range of work for the show, but his was the only art from his hometown. He easily earned his "fifteen minutes of fame." By setting his work in the context of a school of artistic practice, he made a strong impression with the media and visitors to his show. Damian is now the "go-to guy" for the media in his hometown whenever anything visually edgy or experimental comes to town.

Art "stars" or art "novelties" also get press attention. Art stars are artists who are truly original practitioners. They are visionary creators who achieve widespread exposure in important galleries due to their talent; or, they are the dynamic extroverts, the schmoozers extraordinaire, the profoundly talented self-promoters. They are the artists who sell well as a result of an aggressive style.

Being creative in strategizing your media campaign is as important as being creative in the studio. Everyone has amazing stories to tell, it is how they are told that determines whether or not the media takes an interest.

Example: Carly

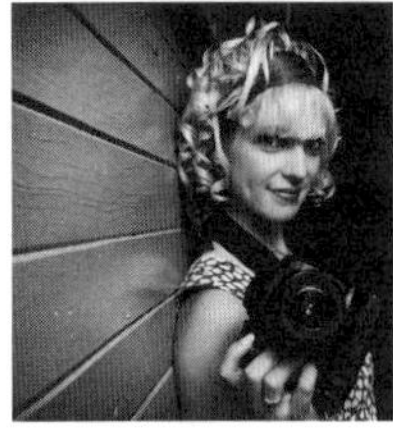

Carly is a photographer. During one stage of her career she toured with rodeo cowboys and documented their life in black and white images. When she showed her work in a local photography gallery, she covered the floor with straw and brought in artifacts from the rodeo—a saddle, gloves, some empty liniment bottles, and handkerchiefs—and she invited some of Canada's best-known professional rodeo cowboys to her opening. Many media representatives attended her show, which subsequently enjoyed popularity in the media and attracted a vastly higher number of visitors than past exhibition openings of the gallery.

Example: Esther

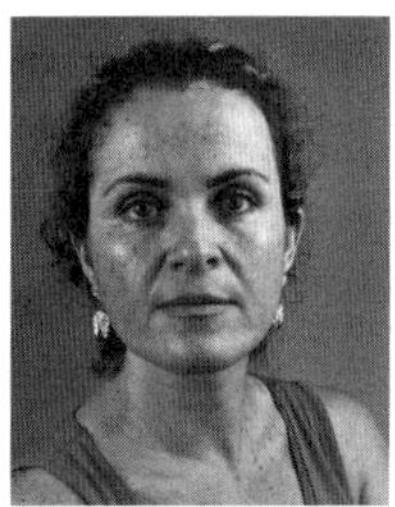

Esther is a printmaker. When she first heard about giclée prints, she had questions. She was curious about how they would affect the marketing and prices of prints made in traditional methods. She was also curious about the permanence of the pigments when giclées started appearing. First, she did all the research she could. Still unable to decide about whether giclée printing was for her or not, she decided to talk with a few local curators who show the work of printmakers and with a local visual arts critic. The critic (at the time) had not heard of giclée prints and was curious about them. At her request, Esther sent the journalist some of her research material. The critic wrote a column about giclée printing and quoted Esther in the article. Many months later, the same critic was writing a story about the impact of new technologies on visual arts education, and she contacted Esther to interview her again. Ever since, Esther has been inviting the critic to her shows; the relationship is building and one day it may lead to a feature article on Esther. In the meantime, her name recognition is growing in the readership of her city's major newspaper.

Following Up

The most important thing to do with a media release is to follow up with telephone calls. A week after you have issued your media release, start calling everyone to whom it was sent (or the most important journalists) to inquire as to whether they received it. If they did, great, ask if you can be of any further assistance. If not, don't start going into things with them, tell them you will get another release to them right away and verify their contact information. The best follow-up is a professional (but warm) call by an effective spokesperson armed with well-written and well-edited support material. Conscripting someone known to journalists—such as a well-known artist, a civil official, or a local celebrity—to do your follow-up can be highly effective

Media & Corporate Sponsorships

Media and corporate sponsorships are based on viewer impressions. The size of your (prospective) audience determines whether or not a media outlet or corporation will consider sponsorship of your event—as will the demographic profile you will have to provide about your expected audience. Collectives stand a chance of attracting crowds in sufficient numbers and therefore qualify for consideration for media sponsorship, but a single artist or small group of artists is unlikely to be as successful. Besides, a media sponsorship is usually out of economic reach of the visual arts—except when in partnership with non-profit organizations with decent budgets. Most media sponsorships involve the sponsor donating media exposure to "top up" exposure purchased by the organization seeking the sponsorship.

If sponsorship is a first-time objective for your event, consult with an arts organization that has negotiated print and/or broadcast media sponsorship (or a corporate sponsorship) in the past. Many media outlets and corporations have information about their sponsorship and philanthropic practices outlined on their websites.

If you are planning an event that will attract a small audience of a common profile (e.g., wealthy people), that may be enough to leverage the sponsorship of a relevant and local small business. Small businesses are often very responsive to an opportunity to meet potential new customers that match their target audience demographics.

ELEVEN

Using the Right Language

"The great enemy of clear language is insincerity. When there is a gap between one's real and one's declared aims, one turns instinctively to long words and exhausted idioms, like a cuttlefish spurting out ink."

—*George Orwell*

"Communication is meaningless without comprehension; visual artists must be sure to use clear language in their marketing and promotional material."

—*C. T.*

The Purpose of Communication

How you communicate is just as important as what you communicate. No matter to whom you are communicating—a prospective dealer, sponsor, buyer, exhibitor, the media, or readers of your website or portfolio—"spelling counts," as our grade-school teachers used to say. So does grammar, neatness, time-sensitivity, and tense agreement—everything counts when you are aiming to make a positive first impression. Besides being accurate, good communication is free of clichés, redundancy, repetition, and jargon. Your communications are a statement about who you are.

You may require a selection of good expository writing, persuasive writing, and advertising copy in your sales and marketing materials to fulfill the textual needs of your career, but writing effectively in all these styles is not something that everyone can do. If this is the case for you, buy, borrow, or barter writing services from someone with experience writing about visual art when you develop your promotional materials.

Artists & Language

Visual artists often think and communicate better in pictures than in words. They are often more comfortable in the tactile and sensate world, as opposed to the heady world of words. As well, artists may lack confidence in writing, preventing them from developing vital text. They may also mistrust language as a result of past experience. Blessed with strength in visual communication, they may have had difficulties in their schooling, where words have ultimate value and pictures have little-to-no academic worth. And language is the medium of criticism—the harshest blows artists may experience may be the words of parents, teachers, or visual art critics. All this "baggage" may make it hard for artists to create effective marketing and self-promotion materials (including the artist statement) that drive readers to the action the artists seek.

Writing about your own work often requires that you analyze every impulse, decision, and motivation. It is work you may not want to do. Any lack of certainty or sense that "I don't matter" or "what I do doesn't matter" will be an obstacle to effective copywriting; or there may be a sense that explaining art is not necessary or that it is anti-art. Artists often say they have nothing to say about their work when they are required to write something about it. At the other end of the scale are those who are impossible to stop talking about their work—both extremes of character can result in the production of weak promotional text if done without professional assistance or careful craftsmanship. All these blocks to the development of effective and persuasive text about you, your art, and your art-making process have to be overcome if you are to develop a successful enterprise around your practice.

Art, Words & Sales

Janine is a Seattle-based artist who recently graduated from art school. Her father, Rob, who had concerns about his daughter's career choice, put pressure on Janine to be practical in her career so that her bills would be sure to be paid.

Rob is a successful advertising executive. He convinced Janine to undertake an experiment as part of her professional development. Following her dad's suggestion, Janine listed the same painting on two charity art-auction websites. One site (Site A) had over 400 bids during the life of their online auction (for all the art in the virtual gallery) and the other site (Site B) had 500 bids. On Site A, Janine titled the piece "Le défunt" (the departed) and wrote about 250 words about her work as being about the personal loss of her best friend. The title on Site B was "Étude en bleu" (study in blue). The description on Site B was ninety-five words about the practice of creating depth through a study in tone.

The highest bid on Site A was $650; the highest bid on Site B was $200. To Rob, this result proved something important: a commodity that involves image-based decision-making has to be "understood" by the buyer, who has to be able to explain why it fits his or her self-image, and so, art must be described. He felt the description on Site A, about loss, made the painting relevant to anyone who has been left or suffered the loss of someone dear. The description of a study in tone is not comprehensible to most people.

Janine said that her father analyzed the correlation of other auction sales with descriptions to further his point about the impact of words on sales. Janine quoted him: "People always have a reason to buy. They either want a work of this dimension for a particular place, or of a certain colour to go with the site palette, because it enhances their self image or because they 'love' it." Because Janine always labeled her work with information about each piece's dimensions and media, Rob felt her shortcoming was not including enough information about its meaning.

Rob's thesis is easy to accept. Everyone is a consumer of products; many of us buy things every day. As consumers, we have expectations, anxieties, desires, and needs. When we are shopping, we want to make the right choice, which is often informed by our own experiences or from obtained information. If we have a choice between two similar products, both of which we like and both are share the same price, but we know a lot about one product and nothing about the other, we will likely choose the product we know something about.

By using effective writing in all your marketing materials, you add value to your work by turning your readers into informed art viewers. By using supplemental text to enhance their viewing experience, it can deepen their emotional reaction to your work, thereby adding to their incentive to buy.

Finding the Right Words

It is rarely advisable to create your marketing materials on your own. You cannot be objective, and you may have a pattern of explaining your work and yourself that is dated and overly subjective. What you need is strongly persuasive or enticing personal text. Choose your style and work on it with professionals if need be. When finding the right words, consider artspeak, adjectives, and using third parties:

1. Artspeak is complex, heavily multi-syllabic text. It is prevalent in some artist statements, curatorial essays, and art criticism. It can alienate some readers as it is can be very hard for them to understand. The language of analysis has its own specialized vocabulary, but the most sophisticated of ideas are also presentable in plain, lay language. When people read your statements, catalogues, website, or media communication, they want contextualization—access to insight, not a serious intellectual challenge. Avoid the jargon of the visual arts if you can.
2. Adjectives are descriptive words that frequently involve judgment;

they go with subjectivity, rather than objectivity. They can be the most dangerous words and they come up often, however; it is hard for a reader to believe adjectives. Consider every adjectival word you use carefully.

3. Using third parties to write or help you to write your marketing materials is highly effective for creating stand-out documents. Some third-party writing methods include: hosting a slide night, which can be an excellent source of raw material for text for your marketing and promotional materials (*see chapter eight*); requesting the assistance of your gallery director (however, beware of text written for you by galleries or dealers—always insist on approval of any text and work with a gallery or professional writer who recognizes the power and value of your voice, not theirs); and requesting the assistance of former teachers, peer artists, art critics, and/or curators (they may provide you with written text free or charge or for a fee).

Some Tips

Have a notebook in your studio or with you when you work. Jot down ideas and insights that occur as you work. Try to explain what your work is about in a short paragraph or two, and build it up over time. Is your work about your ideas, your life events, or a philosophic value or belief? Is it part of a narrative expressed in a body of work? Do you know where you will end up when you start a piece, or does it shape its destiny with you as you work? How do you know when to stop, or when it is done? Use your notebook to annotate your behavioral and mental creative process. Discover and record why you make art—your reasons may change over time or from day to day. The clearer you are about your drive to create, the better for you and your marketing materials. Also consider: where do you work? Why do you work? Who are your influences? What emotions drive you to create? How do you feel when a work sells? What are your other passions? As previously mentioned, people invest in artists, not art, so personal details, although they may not seem important to you, may be interesting to your potential buyers.

Don't preach or write too much. Avoid superlatives and ensure every word is important. Read and re-read your work, eliminating all ambiguities and extraneous text.

Read aloud. One of the best ways any writer can test her or his work is to read it aloud. Reading text that you think is finished aloud to someone is a very effective way to do some self-editing—even reading it aloud to yourself is also worthwhile. Never print, publish, or email anything important that has not been proofread or read aloud.

Persuasive Writing

The biggest challenge for artists can be the need for effective, persuasive copywriting that requires the writer to take a position for or against something; the writers want to convince the readers to believe in something or to do something. Persuasive writing should be in your sales and marketing materials and in letters to solicit gallery representation, an exhibition, a sponsor, or a grant. Here are some guidelines to help you develop effective persuasive text.

Persuasive writing usually follows a particular format— introduction, body, and conclusion. The introduction is designed to demand the reader's attention. You can do that by beginning your copy with:

1. Something striking or unusual: "Perhaps never before have cow placentas been used as an artistic medium" (as was the case in a Vancouver Artropolis exhibition).
2. A provocative statement: "Most modern art is soulless."
3. A quotation: an excerpted line from an art critic or a curator, properly credited, is highly effective.
4. A statistic or impressive fact: "This year I had more exhibitions and sold more work that in any other year of my career."
5. An anecdote that is brief, relevant, and interesting (or amusing) can be a good soft opening: "Goldie Hawn, known for her excellent taste, recently bought some of my work."
6. A question: "Do you know why so many people bought the art of [your name] last year?"
7. Hyperbole (be careful here): "Critics are calling [your name] someone to watch!"

Besides the opening "grab," your introduction will make your thesis clear for the reader. Your opening paragraph should tell the reader exactly what your purpose is and how you are going to prove it. The opening paragraph is an extremely short forecasting of the rest of your text. Here is an example: "Perhaps no other artist has so engaged Vancouver gallery-goers as [your name]. [*Engaging opening statement.*] A review of [your] exhibition reviews and publications, and a look at who is buying [his/her] art proves that [you] are an excellent investment for the discerning art buyer! [*Thesis statement.*]"

Next comes the body of your text, where you address your thesis. This is where you elaborate. You want clear, enticing, and convincing text. You want to create confidence in your reader by proving your thesis in an engaging, believable, and interesting way. Each paragraph should concisely and convincingly elaborate on a single solid reason that supports your thesis statement. Provide background information a reader may need and provide illustrations if, and whenever, it is appropriate. Do not duplicate imagery or information used in your other marketing materials to which the reader might refer. Define any specialized terms that you use, and cue your reader when necessary (e.g., "first," "second"; "next," "then"). Draw comparisons when appropriate to assist in supporting your thesis, showing images by artists who have influenced you, for example.

Close your text with a conclusion. A good conclusion may summarize the main points made in the body of your text that conclusively proves the thesis (repeating the thesis), or you may close with a differently worded statement used in your opening. More than anything, however, effective persuasive marketing text ends with a call for action—that is, motivation to buy your work, attend your show, or give you a grant.

Again, for effective, persuasive copywriting:

1. Have a thesis (a point of view) for the reader to accept.
2. Begin with an attention-getting opening statement.
3. Provide evidence proving the thesis.
4. End with a summary and call for action.

Public Speaking

The volume and pace at which you speak, the language that you use, how much eye contact you offer those to whom you are speaking and your comfort level will all affect your audience. Unless you are a natural public speaker or have taken a course on public speaking, you will benefit from practice if, and when, you are called upon to speak about your art.

Text for a public oral presentation can be extrapolated from your marketing materials. You will rarely need to develop new text, but live speech should be in the first person, so minor changes may be required.

Many artists, when called upon to speak, like to ad lib. This may be a technique that works for some, but it rarely is as effective as something planned. If you want to make the best possible presentation, consider this method:

1. Collect all the points you want to make from your promotional materials, diary, and from any reviews, publications, and third-party copy. Put your points into an interesting order that logically flows from point to point.
2. Add a welcoming comment and some acknowledgment comments (of guests, special guests, helpers, hosts, etc.) at the beginning of your series of points to make, and have "thank you" comments at the end.
3. Next, on small cards (three by five inches), write in large type and in simple language a single point per one card, then put all your cards in order, from "welcome" to "thank you and good night." An excellent tip used by good speakers, is to add cards that provide an effective segue or transition from one point to the next.
4. If you want to appear casual when making your speech, use each card as a base for improvising your actual words. This allows you to take in each point at a glance and quickly move the card to the back so your next point is immediately visible, and it means you can maintain eye contact with the public through most of your speech.
5. If you are nervous about public speaking, write out your whole speech in large type on 8.5- by 11-inch sheets. Before you present the speech, however, read it aloud several times at home so that parts come easily to you. Also, consider printing your speech so that each paragraph changes colour. Doing so makes it easy for you to remember where you are when you look up to make eye contact and return to your text to read.

6. When you deliver your speech, do so slowly—very slowly and with inflection when appropriate. Pause at the end of sentences. Allow your points to sink in and make eye contact with your audience in your pauses and whenever you can—especially when you move from one page to the next. The large type helps you read your speech easily.
7. If you are nervous, saying so as part of your speech can often help you relax and it can turn your audience from potential critics to empathetic supporters.
8. Humour relaxes everyone.
9. Be as brief as you can be while ensuring that you make all relevant points. Time your presentation when you test read it aloud. Keep within the time guidelines of your host and leave time for questions.

Cover Letters

Artists will often have to write letters of request—for an exhibition, to be represented, for a grant or commission, or in response to a public call for entry. Your letters should be clear, having precise language that immediately and exclusively addresses the need. They should reveal that you are knowledgeable, mirroring and addressing the language and expectations of the letters' addressees.

When you are responding to a call for entry, your letters should address the terms of involvement or objectives of the call, why you are an ideal candidate, and conclude with a sincere expression of thanks for their time taken in considering your application. Your response can be passionate in its conviction that you have the skills and experience to meet the needs of the addressee, but it should be focused and efficient. Good cover letters do not repeat information contained in the portfolio. They engage the recipient by speaking directly to the call's requirements. And remember, the proof of you being the ideal candidate is in your support material, not in the cover letter.

TWELVE

Tax Considerations for Artists

"Next to being shot at and missed, nothing is really quite as satisfying as an income tax refund." —*F. J. Raymond*

"Artists that produce and market their art and artistic talents fall within the generic category of 'small business' and this category contains the greatest number of business entities in the country."

—*Robert McMurray*

Introduction

Robert McMurray is the author of this chapter. He is a fellow of the Institute of Chartered Accountants of British Columbia and also a signature member (AFCA) of the Federation of Canadian Artists, its past president, and a member of their board of directors. He has been painting and exhibiting for over thirty years.

Taxation is an important consideration for the self-employed artist/small businessperson. If you find aspects of this chapter challenging, it should reinforce Robert's advice to engage a tax advisor or accountant.

The advice presented in the chapter is accurate at the time of printing. Please refer to *artistsurvivalskills.com* to see if any information presented here has been updated due to changes in legislation or Canada Revenue Agency policy interpretation.

This chapter is technical in that is deals with specifics of the Income Tax Act. The information is provided for you to use if you do your own taxes or for you to provide to your accountant if he or she is not experienced with tax law interpretation for visual artists.

When filing income taxes, artists who produce and market their work and artistic talents fall within the generic category of "small business"; this category contains the greatest number of business entities in the country. Most of these small businesses have five or fewer employees and account for

Example: Chris

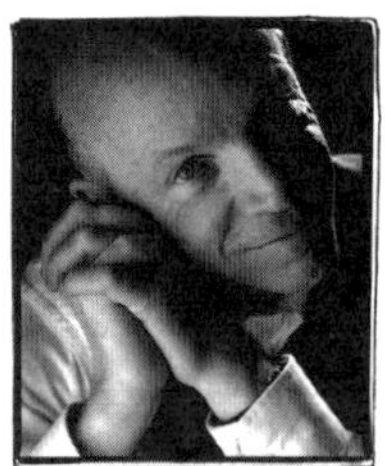

Chris traditionally did his own taxes. Each year, he received a modest tax return (about $200). As a salaried employee in a "day job," he earned decent self-employed income as an artist. The first time he had an accountant do his taxes for him, his annual tax return increased ten-fold ($2,000). The cost of his accountant was $800, so he was left with far more cash in his pocket than when he did his taxes himself. His accountant helped him set up his system of record keeping, and he's never done his taxes since. Be an artist—hire an accountant!

a significant portion of private sector jobs; many of which are occupied by self-employed individuals with no employees.

Most of the issues and decisions you will face at tax time are common to all small businesses. However, there are a few options that are only available to artists; they are identified in this chapter.

Have a Tax Advisor

It is strongly recommended that you find a qualified income tax advisor to assist you in the preparation and filing of your income tax returns. If you don't have someone in mind, ask for a recommendation from other artists in business who work with one. You can keep the cost down by doing your own record keeping and presenting your summary of transactions and questions to your advisor. Alternatively, you can study the laws and look after these matters yourself. You are better off doing what you do well, and leaving the tax work to professionals who are up to date on the rules and their practical application.

What follows is an outline of Canadian federal tax issues and business matters to consider as a self-employed artist. The tax regulations mentioned are current as of the time of writing (updates will be posted on *artistsurvivalskills.com*). Provincial tax laws vary from one province to another; check the pertinent tax law in your province of residence if you are doing your taxes yourself.

Reporting or Not?

Here are some considerations to make before filing a federal income tax return:

1. If you are earning taxable income, reporting it is not an option—you must report your income in your tax return.
2. If your revenues are less than your expenses, you may not need to report your income in your tax return, but in certain circumstances it is optional (the definition of income includes "loss").
3. If you are making ends meet through outside employment, it will likely be to your advantage to deduct your business loss from your employment income to reduce your taxable income.

Determining If You Are a Business

In order to deduct losses, you must meet two requirements as established by the Stewart case (*Stewart v. Canada*, 2002 SCC 46, [2002] 2 S.C.R. 645). You must be carrying on a business and you must be in pursuit of profit.

The Canada Revenue Agency (CRA) applies a set of criteria known as the REOP (reasonable expectation of profit) test and these are set out in Interpretation Bulletin IT 504R2 (*see appendix X or website*). The REOP test indicates to the CRA whether or not you are in business and can deduct your tax losses from your other income. The IT 504R2 also states that you need not meet all of the criteria, but should meet a reasonable number of them. The ruling in the Stewart case indicated that the REOP test is not the primary test and should only be applied when there is a personal element in the business. Job satisfaction is not considered a personal element. However, IT 504R2 is a good checklist to use to determine how the CRA would look at your business activities.

In summary, the REOP test considers:

1. The time devoted to the business.
2. Whether your work is presented in public and private settings.
3. Whether a gallery or an agent represents you.
4. The type of activity and time spent in promoting and marketing work.
5. The amounts of your revenues and the progress in your prices.
6. Your history of profits and losses.
7. The progress in the value and popularity of your works.
8. The type and relevance of your expenditures.
9. Your qualifications, education, and recognition.

The IT 504R2 recognizes that artists may take longer than the average business to reach a profitable stage and that they may not sell a painting for a very long time.

What Revenue to Report

When reporting your revenue, it is important to note:

1. Revenues must be accounted for on a "calendar year" basis.
2. There are a number of provisions for partial business years, such as when you start up a business part way through the calendar year.

The main provisions deal with capital cost allowance (depreciation) on capital assets (studio equipment, computer, car, etc.). Capital assets are those that cost over $200 and have a useful life of more than one year.

3. Revenues include the following: sales of your service or product, fees for services, fees for workshops, lectures, and demonstrations, and deemed sales.

   Deemed sales can be:

   Trades for goods or services (barter)—you must include in income the fair market value of your goods or services disposed of in trade. If the goods or services that you receive in trade are used in your business, you can include the same amount in your expenses or capital cost additions.

   Donations of goods or services to a registered charity—you must include in income the fair market value of your goods or services in your income, but you can claim the equivalent donation receipt in your non-refundable tax credits. (There is a special election available to artists that will be dealt with in the next section.)

   Donations to unregistered charities—again, include the fair market value in your revenues, and if the goods or services that you receive in trade are used in your business, you can include the same amount in your expenses or capital cost additions.

4. Special election available to artists for donation of artworks to registered charitable organizations: you may designate a number between zero and the fair market value of the donated artwork, and that number will apply to both the deemed revenue and to the donation credit claimed. If you are not in the top tax bracket, it will likely be to your advantage to use the full fair market value amount (the deemed revenue is taxed at your marginal tax rate and the tax credit on aggregate donations in excess of $200 is calculated at the highest tax rate). The donation tax credit is completely offset by the additional tax if your taxable income has reached the top tax bracket (at approximately $120,000).

What Expenses to Claim

When claiming expenses on your income tax return, the bottom line is: be reasonable and keep your records. Here are the allowable expenses to claim:

1. **All non-capital amounts** expended for the purpose of earning income. Capital assets are those that cost over $200 and have a useful life of more than one year.
2. **The cost of travel** to gather subject or reference material to be used in creating your artwork. These expenses include transportation, lodging, meals, entertainment, taxis, gratuities, and relevant admission fees such as those to museums or art galleries.
3. **Meals and entertainment** ("entertainment" means alcohol): record these amounts including tips, if any. You can claim 50% of these expenses and there is a calculation for this adjustment in the income tax return itself.
4. **Cash expenses**: keep receipts for these and if you forget to get one or one is not issued, then note, in ink on a piece of paper, the date, payee, amount, and purpose of the expenditure and include this note with your other receipts and vouchers.
5. **If the main purpose** of the trip is for business, but it includes some non-business time (e.g., visiting relatives), then apportion the expenses on some reasonable basis and keep your notes as to how you arrived at that apportionment.

Capital Expenditures

Capital expenditure claims include any item costing more than $200 that is useful for more than one year. They must be capitalized (set aside in a depreciable asset account) and amortized or depreciated by claiming capital cost allowance (CCA) over a number of years. They are also pooled by class or category, and their CCA rates are as follows:

Class 1 is for buildings: acquired before March 20, 2007—4%; acquired after March 19, 2007—6%

Class 6 is for buildings acquired for manufacturing or processing use: acquired before March 20, 2007—4%; acquired after March 19, 2007—10%

Class 8 is for equipment and furnishings and for small tools costing more than $500—20%

Class 10 is for automobiles costing less than $30,000 excluding taxes—30% on $30,000

Class 10.1 is for passenger vehicles costing more than $30,000, excluding taxes

Class 12 includes computer software—100%

Class 12 includes small tools and equipment costing less than $500—100%

Class 45 is for computer hardware acquired before March 20, 2007—45%

Class 45.1 is for computer hardware acquired after March 19, 2007—55%

These CCA rates may change from time to time or you may have assets in other classes, so it is a good idea to consult your tax advisor, the CRA information line, or the Government of Canada website (*canada.gc.ca*) to be sure that you are using the appropriate CCA rates.

There is a "half year" rule requiring that you can only claim half the normal capital cost allowance or amortization in the year of acquisition. The CCA schedules in the tax forms provide for this adjustment.

The capital cost allowance is calculated on the "declining balance" method, wherein you deduct the first year claim from the balance in the pool and in the next year, you add the cost of any additions, deduct the proceeds of any disposals, and then calculate the CCA on the remaining balance. The CCA is then deducted to arrive at an underappreciated capital cost of the pool at the end of the year, which is then carried into the beginning of the next year. You then add the cost of any additions for that year, deduct the proceeds of any disposals, and then calculate the CCA on the remaining balance (and so on).

If the balance in the pool becomes negative at the end of the year, usually through dispositions, you must take that amount into income as recaptured CCA since the CCA claimed over the years was greater than the actual loss of value. You can recapture the CCA claimed, up to the original cost of the asset, and any excess represents a capital gain, 50% of which is subject to income tax.

Employing Family Members

If family members (e.g., spouse, children, or parents) work in your business, you can pay them reasonable wages based on the value of the services that they perform for you. This is a business expense for you and employment income for the family member(s). You should keep a detailed job description for each family member employed, describing the different services that they perform for your business and arrange for standard payroll deductions that apply (income tax and Canada Pension). Employment Insurance also applies but may not apply in the case of your spouse; consult your tax advisor or the Canada Revenue Agency information services.

"Change-In-Use" Inventory

This provision allows you to account for the supplies and capital items that you have on hand on the day that you commence your business. You are considered to have sold these items and reacquired them at the lower of cost or fair market value on that date. You must prepare a detailed inventory or listing of everything that you have acquired up to that date and are carrying forward into the business accounts, including:

1. Art and studio supplies.
2. Saleable work and products.
3. Studio equipment and furniture.
4. Computer software and computer equipment and peripherals.
5. Photo reference material.
6. Reference library.
7. Any other item used in your process.

You should list and identify the major items and group smaller items (tubes of paint, brushes, etc.) and retain this inventory listing as part of your permanent records.

Business-in-the-Home Expenses

If you are using part of your home in which to carry on your business, you can claim reasonable expenses for that portion (see the IT 514 tax bulletin). You cannot claim for common or shared space (e.g., dining room, kitchen, or bathroom). However, if one of these spaces were used exclusively for business purposes then it would be appropriate to include it in the business area. To determine the portion of the home that is being used for business, measure the business space in relation to the total area of the home.

It is generally not to your advantage to claim capital cost allowance (CCA) on the portion of the structure that is used for business since the CCA rates are very low. This includes anything that is attached to the structure (e.g., shelving, flooring, built-ins, or lights). It does not include freestanding shelving, unattached rugs, and freestanding lighting.

You can claim the business portion of property taxes, insurance, utilities, garbage disposal, rent, and any other expenses that can be attributed to your business area. Business-in-the-home expenses may be claimed against income earned from the home-based business, but they cannot be used to create or enlarge a loss. Any unused business-in-the-home expenses that cannot be claimed in the year may be accumulated and carried forward indefinitely to apply against future income from the business in the home.

Motor Vehicle Operating Expenses

Keep a record of all operating expenses and the appropriate receipts—fuel, servicing, repairs, tires, car lease, financing interest, and insurance. Keep a log showing, for each business trip, the date, kilometres traveled, and purpose of the trip, as well as incidental expenses incurred (parking, meals, ferry fares, etc.). The log is your proof of the portion of expenses that you are claiming for business purposes. You don't have to write down the starting and ending odometer readings for every trip—use your trip meter. You'll find that you have quite a few standard trips and the distance will be the same every time so you only need to measure it once. Note the opening and closing odometer readings for the year to determine total kilometres traveled in the year. This information will allow you to calculate your total operating expenses, including the CCA on your vehicle and prorate them in the ratio of your business kilometres to your total kilometres for the year.

Year-End Inventories

Businesses are required to go through an inventory process at the end of each year in order to match expenses to the revenues generated in the year (see the IT 473R tax bulletin). The calculation requires them to take stock of all unsold or unused material at the end of the year, value this inventory at the lower of cost or realizable value, and deduct this value from the expenses for the year. The expenses for the year include the value of the prior year's closing inventory carried into the current year, plus the cost of expenditures during the year. This process matches the revenues against the cost of generating those revenues and gives a reasonably accurate picture of the profit for the year.

Artists have an option available to them that other businesses do not, in that they may elect to apply zero value or nil for the year-end inventory. In this case, the expenses of the year are written off in the year, making for much simpler accounting. Artists should elect this method in the process of filing a tax return for the first year of operation. Once either inventory method is elected, it cannot easily be changed and any change would require approval of the CRA.

Goods & Services Tax

A goods and services tax (GST) exemption is available if your small business's gross revenues are less than $30,000 in the calendar year. Using this exemption, you would not register for GST, you would pay GST on all expenses and you would not charge GST on your sales or revenues. If, however, at any time during the calendar year your gross revenues or sales reach $30,000, you must register for GST and charge GST on your revenues or sales thereafter. You are required to keep a running tally of your revenues/sales if you are getting close to that mark. Registration is optional if your revenues/sales are under $30,000 in a year. If you do register, you would charge GST on all domestic revenues/sales and you would claim a credit for all GST paid on operating and capital expenses.

It may be to your advantage to register for GST as soon as you commence business: firstly, the GST collected is over and above your normal revenues and secondly, the GST paid on expenses is deducted from that collected and only the balance is remitted. In effect, your recover the GST on expenses. If you are registered and selling your product through a reseller (store or gallery), provide them with your registration number and they must pay you the GST on your share of any sale proceeds.

You may have a choice in registering for GST as to how frequently you will file GST returns—quarterly, semiannually, or annually. Filing quarterly ensures that you don't leave it all to the end of the year, making it much easier to maintain—doing your record keeping, paying the tax if a balance is owing, or receiving a refund if your GST paid exceeds your GST collected. In addition, if your revenues are robust, quarterly reporting means not having a big GST bill to pay at the end of the year.

Provincial Sales Taxes/Harmonized Sales Tax

A number of provinces have a provincial sales tax (PST), and others have tied their sales taxes to the GST reports as harmonized sales tax (HST). If you are conducting a business in a province with PST or HST, you should get advice from your tax advisor on the registration requirements and options.

Record Keeping

Record keeping need not be overly complicated. The objective is to record your revenues, operating expenses, and capital transactions in a way that will give you the annual totals for each type of transaction and provide an easy-to-follow trail that goes back to the supporting documentation (invoices, receipts, deposit slips, cheques, and your bank account). This facilitates answering any questions that may arise regarding your income tax returns and supports the figures that you have used in filing returns.

The simplest system is manual and uses a series of envelopes, one for each type of revenue and expense, and for capital items. You label the envelope for the type of transaction, write the amount on the outside, and put the documentation in the envelope. At the end of the year, all you have to do is add up the figures on each envelope and make a summary of the envelopes' titles and totals. Transfer the information to the appropriate part of your tax form or send the summary to your accountant (retaining the receipts for your records).

A little bit more complicated is a manual bookkeeping system where, instead of using envelopes, you use a columnar journal. In your journal, you list all your bank and cash transactions, entering the corresponding amounts in the appropriate columns that are entitled with the same titles as the envelopes. The supporting documentation is then filed in an order that allows you to find the documentation easily from looking at the journal (e.g., cheque numbers). If you are familiar with spreadsheet programs, such as Excel or Lotus 123, you can put the same information on a spreadsheet as you would in a journal and automate some of the tax calculations by using formulae.

Even more complicated and more costly (the software) is using one of the many accounting programs available. This method has a learning curve, but may be simplified if you or a family member has experience with the software. These programs have the advantage, if they are kept up to date, of seeing what your income and expense account looks like at any time in the year. This is particularly useful if you are having a good year and can benefit from some tax planning before year-end. (Two very popular programs for small business are QuickBooks and Simply Accounting that cost in the range of $150 to $200.)

You should package and label your records annually and retain them for at least seven years. The Canada Revenue Agency can open up a file for audit up to three years after the date of assessment for the year. If you file a tax return for the 2007 year in May of 2008 and it is assessed on June 20 2008, the CRA has until June 20, 2011 to open the file for audit should they wish to do so. You should retain, indefinitely, the records of assets that you still hold (such as stocks, vehicles, and property) so that you can prove cost in any capital gain or loss calculations when such assets are sold.

You don't require permission to destroy old records, so each year you can take the oldest package beyond the seven years and destroy it. If you are registered for GST and PST/HST, your record keeping will need additional columns or accounts for GST collected, GST paid, and PST/HST collected.

Incorporation

Incorporating your small business offers the following advantages:

1. It is a separate legal entity with an infinite life as long as the proper annual reports are filed.
2. Generally, the amount of liability of the corporation is limited to the value of the corporation's assets.
3. Small business corporations enjoy a lower income tax rate than individuals and therefore have more after-tax income to re-invest in business capital assets or working capital.

4. It provides the illusion of a larger business.
5. It allows a certain measure of smoothing income over fat and lean years, providing more stable personal taxes.

Incorporation, however, also has the following drawbacks:

1. There are more onerous financial and compliance reporting requirements, so annual accounting and legal costs are higher.
2. It is a more complicated form of business.
3. Incorporation will not save or defer personal income taxes if all of the income flows through to the principal shareholder(s) each year. The lower tax rate applies only to income left in the corporation for re-investment.

Additional Information

See Interpretation Bulletin IT 525R relating to performing artists for more information. See Appendix G for information on how to access Interpretation Bulletins referred to in this chapter.

Also, the Canada Revenue Agency has a number of publications available for small businesses that are available either online or in hard copy at most local tax offices; look the office up in the blue pages and phone first to make sure they are in stock.

13

Copyrights & Appropriation

"In vain we call old notions fudge,
And bend our conscience to our dealing;
The Ten Commandments will not budge,
And stealing will continue stealing.

— *James Russell Lowell*
(Motto of the American Copyright League)

"Canadian visual artists need never worry about their copyrights thanks to CARFAC and its Collective." — *C. T.*

Introduction

Copyright is an important issue for visual artists. The visual artist's copyrights are multifaceted and technical. Only a light overview of the subject is presented here because Canadian visual artists can both learn in depth about their copyrights and protect them through the organization, Canadian Artists' Representation/Le Front des artistes canadiens (CARFAC), and their subsidiary, Copyright Collective (CARCC). By joining the CARCC, you support Canada's foremost and practical support service organization for visual artists; by working in partnership with the CARCC, you protect your copyrights.

What Is CARFAC?

The Canadian Artists' Representation was founded in London, Ontario, when a group of artists, headed by Jack Chambers, organized themselves to collectively demand recognition of their copyrights. They began issuing minimum copyright fee schedules, and they continue to produce them regularly. All fees are considered minimum payments for the use of the copyrights and/or the professional services of visual and media artists.

CARFAC has had a long history of involvement in the evolution of copyright legislation in Canada. Most significantly, in 1988, their lobbying efforts facilitated the federal Copyright Act Amendment that recognizes artists as the primary producers of culture, and enables artists to receive exhibition and other fees related to their copyrighted work.

The following text is from the CARFAC website (www.carfac.ca):

> "CARFAC is incorporated federally as a non-profit corporation that is the national voice of Canada's professional visual artists. As a non-profit association and a National Art Service Organization, our mandate is to promote the visual arts in Canada, to promote a socio-economic climate that is conducive to the production of visual arts in Canada, and to conduct research and engage in public education for these purposes.
>
> CARFAC was established by artists in 1968 and has been recognized by the *Status of the Artist* legislation; CARFAC is guided by an active Board, elected by the membership.

We believe that artists, like professionals in other fields, should be paid for their work and share equitably in profits from their work. As the national voice of Canada's professional visual artists, CARFAC defends artists' economic and legal rights and educates the public on fair dealing with artists. In doing so, CARFAC promotes a socio-economic climate conducive to the production of visual arts. CARFAC engages actively in advocacy, lobbying, research and public education on behalf of artists in Canada."

What Is the CARFAC Copyright Collective?

The following text is from the Copyright Collective section of the CARFAC website:

"CARCC (Canadian Artists Representation Copyright Collective Inc), established in 1990, is a copyright collective that licenses and administers copyright for visual and media artists in Canada. [It] is a subsidiary organization of CARFAC [....]

Affiliates or members of CARCC assign their copyrights to CARCC for licensing and administration. All uses of a CARCC member's copyright must be licensed by CARCC.

Some of the copyrights administered by CARCC are: exhibition, reproduction, reprography and telecommunication. In addition to representing living artists, CARCC represents artists' estates. In Canada, most copyrights endure for the artist's lifetime plus fifty years. Moral rights endure for the same length of time.

Copyright fees are increasingly becoming a necessary and major source of income for visual artists. Copyright is not transferred upon the sale of a work; copyright is retained by the artist unless specifically and separately sold, and the artist can continue to generate copyright revenue from the work after the work itself is sold or donated."

What Are Artists' Rights?

The following information is also from the CARFAC website:

1. Exhibition rights involve "the right to present the work for a public exhibition, for a purpose other than for sale or hire."

2. Reproduction rights involve "the right to reproduce the work, or any substantial part thereof, in any material or electronic form, by means now or hereafter known."
3. Reprography rights involve "the right to make visually perceivable copies of published works by such means as photocopy, duplication (by stencil), microfilm or transcription for overhead slide projection."
4. Telecommunication Rights involve "the right to use a work on radio or television and the right to transmission of a work via cable, satellite and telephone wires. This also includes the right to the retransmission of the same work."
5. Moral Rights are rights that "remain with the creator/author even if the copyright is assigned to another party. The artist's reputation is protected through rights of Paternity, integrity and association."

You can also learn more about all these rights on the CARFAC website (*carfac.ca*), including information about the services the CARCC offers to individual artists; forms, such as fees for artists' rights, available for downloading, as well as agreements and membership application; a sample artist's résumé; and information about the implications of copyright on the artist's estate.

Defending Your Copyrights

Should your rights be violated to the extent that you feel forced to defend them, it will likely be a frustrating, expensive, and an unfulfilling experience for you if it involves lawyers. Do anything and everything possible to prevent yourself from having to settle an infringement case in the court system—attempt to find solutions through mediation and/or arbitration before you consider litigation.

In 1997, Sally felt that another artist had infringed her copyrights. She could not find a satisfactory solution to the problem through discussions with the offending artist, so she hired a lawyer to seek redress. She won her case, but at a tremendous financial and emotional cost to both parties. Her case is one of several that have no winners.

Nothing has caused more of a stir about copyrights that the phenomena of "poaching." Poachers steal your designs from online postings of your art that they find on your website, blog, or virtual gallery, and then have them reproduced in their homeland. Several Vancouver artists worked together to defeat such an operation, but pursuing the violation of copyrights in another country and in a foreign language proved barely effective and very expensive. Their energy was redirected to the media in hopes of saving other artists from suffering the same fate. Now, many of these artists imbed "watermarks" in their online images as a step toward preventing piracy.

Appropriation

Appropriation is an increasingly dangerous practice. Artists considering this practice should be wary. Appropriating something involves "taking possession" of it. Stealing is appropriating, and so is borrowing (with or without permission), and so are "referencing" and "sampling." In the visual arts, the term is applied to the tradition of using borrowed elements in the creation of new work. Artists appropriate both historical and contemporary images, shapes, and styles.

Appropriation has a long history in the visual arts. In its essence, the making of much visual art is an appropriating activity inasmuch as artistic creation often involves the interpretation or stylization of imagery or ideas taken from the world that we live in. Shakespeare appropriated the plots of many of his plays, but he retold the stories in a unique and masterful way. His genius of expression is what made his versions of the stories endure.

Art historians credit Pablo Picasso and Georges Braque as the modern founders of the appropriation movement in modern visual art. They are credited as being the first to appropriate "non-art" images into their work. Picasso used newspaper imagery extensively to create new work; both used items from our "real" world on their canvases as early as 1912.

In 1917, Marcel Duchamp achieved fame through his *Fountain* entry in an exhibition of the American Society of Independent Artists. The piece was a urinal on its side mounted on a pedestal and bearing the signature "R. Mutt." He also used a copy of the *Mona Lisa* in his work, *L.H.O.O.Q.* Duchamp was a Dadaist and many of his colleagues in the movement appropriated quotidian objects; the surrealists brought the term "found object" into the visual arts vocabulary.

In the 1950s, Robert Rauschenberg and Jasper Johns utilized found objects. Johns' appropriation of the target image and the American flag are as well known as Andy Warhol's appropriation of the Campbell's soup can. The Fluxus art movement appropriated the postal system in creating and popularizing mail art; and "pop" artists appropriated advertising, trademark, and comic book imagery in their work. But it wasn't until the 1980s that the term entered the common vocabulary of visual artists. Perhaps no better examples of appropriation are the images of Walker Evans that occur in the work of American artist Sherrie Levine.

In all these cases, the appropriating artists use the appropriated image to further their creative statement. They contextualize the appropriated image in order to make unique creative statements. Recognition of the appropriation is an important part of the work—it is not concealed; it is acknowledged. Copyright infringement, on the other hand, involves unacknowledged reproduction.

If you are planning on referencing or appropriating imagery in your artwork, do so legally, by contributing significantly to its context so as to ensure you have a sound legal and artistic rationale for its use. You can consult with other artists, curators, or professors of art easily via the web and email.

There are very contentious issues in the appropriation art field. To learn more about it, visit the blog, Appropriation Art (*appropriationart.ca*).

Appropriation Art, CARFAC, and CARCC are concerned with protecting the "referencing" tradition in art while, at the same time, honouring the rights of visual art creators.

At the time of writing, CARFAC Ontario is working with CARFAC (national) on the development of an "Advisory Note" on appropriation. CARFAC's head office and two of its regional branches in Ontario and Saskatchewan have hosted public panels on the issue. In the spring of 2007, CARFAC published articles on appropriation and copyright in their newsletter, which can be found on their website.

Additional Information

Updates on the issues of copyright and appropriation will be posted on *artistsurvivalskills.com*.

Canadian Artists Representation Copyright Collective Inc.
109A Fourth Avenue,
Ottawa, ON K1S 2L3
Telephone: (613) 232-3818; Fax: (613) 232-8384
Toll free: 866-502-2722; Email: *carcc@carcc.ca*

14

Health & Safety and Estate Planning

"The truly creative mind in any field is no more than this: A human creature born abnormally, inhumanly sensitive. To him ... a touch is a blow, a sound is a noise, a misfortune is a tragedy, a joy is an ecstasy, a friend is a lover, a lover is a god, and failure is death. Add to this cruelly delicate organism the overpowering necessity to create, create, create—so that without the creating of music or poetry or books or buildings or something of meaning, his very breath is cut off from him. He must create, must pour out creation. By some strange, unknown, inward urgency he is not really alive unless he is creating."

— *Pearl S. Buck, (1892–1973),*
Novelist and Nobel laureate

"The one important thing I have learned over the years is the difference between taking one's work seriously and taking one's self seriously. The first is imperative and the second is disastrous."

— *Dame Margot Fontaine*

Health & Safety

Without you, your business does not grow; every sick day sets you back. Because many artists work with toxic materials or use materials that pollute the environment without proper containment, and because some artists have issues with repetitive use injuries and weakened immune systems, all artists are wise to consider their practice with a concern for their safety and wellbeing. This book cannot be a health manual; instead, some resources are listed below.

Websites

Environmental Defence (*environmentaldefence.ca/toxicnation*) this site includes topics entitled Artists' Toxic Illnesses, Artists at Special Risk, Toxic Hazards in Your Studio, Defense Against Toxic Materials, The Healthy Artist Guide to a Less Toxic Studio, Staying Alive!—Health and Safety Workshops for Visual and Media Artists, and Toxic Nation Fact Sheet.

CARFAC Ontario (carfacontario.ca/about/health_and_safety): CARFAC Ontario has developed The Online Health & Safety Store "to provide easy access to resources and help artists understand the importance of safe studio practices." (CARFAC Ontario, 440–401 Richmond St. West, Toronto, ON, M5V 1P9; Tel: 416-340-8850 or toll-free: 877-890-8850 email: *carfacontario@carfacontario*)

Publications

***Health Hazards Manual for Artists* by Michael McCann** (Revised edition. The Lyons Press, 2004): this book is a benchmark resource for visual artists. It details harmful effects caused by art materials and procedures that can make working with these materials safer.

Making Art Safely: Alternative Methods and Materials in Drawing, Painting, Printmaking, Graphic Design, and Photography *by Merle Spandorfer, Deborah Curtiss, and Jack Snyder* *(John Wiley & Sons, 1995):* this book identifies hazardous materials and techniques that are commonly used in art. It demonstrates safe alternatives through text and step-by-step illustrations.

***The Artist's Complete Health and Safety Guide* by Monona Rossol** (Third edition. Allworth Press, 2001).

"The Healthy Artist Guide to a Less Toxic Studio" (Environmental Defence and CARFAC Ontario; see *carfacontario.ca*)

"Health Hazards in the Arts" (Rochester Institute of Technology; see *wally.rit.edu/pubs/guides/healthhaz*)

Health Centre

Al & Malka Green Artists' Health Centre: The AHC is part of the Healthy Connections Program at Toronto Western Hospital (see *uhn.ca*). The Centre offers complementary, alternative, and conventional health care to professional creative and performing artists, and to students and staff at post-secondary arts institutions. The Centre's mandate includes research, education, and outreach to the arts community. (The Al & Malka Green Artists' Health Centre, Toronto Western Hospital, Third Floor, West Wing, 399 Bathurst St, Toronto, ON, M5T 2S8; Tel: 416-603-5263)

Dealing with Rejection

The first (and often worst) sense of rejection an artist feels sometimes comes from family and/or school when she or he first expresses a passion for visual expression and a career in the arts. This is often not a choice that is welcomed by those on whom we rely for support; it can be the first test of the artist's conviction. But many more tests will follow. With luck or hard work, artists can use each rejection to strengthen the resolution to create.

Every time visual artists submit their work for the consideration of a gallery owner, curator, buyer, jury, admission panel, professor, friend, neighbour, and (above all) our fellow artists, one of three things will happen: they will get a positive response, a negative response, or a neutral (balanced or mixed) response. Their chances of getting either praise or outright rejection are 33%, but their chances of not getting praise at all are 66%.

Over a lifetime, artists can receive a lot of rejection; cumulative rejection can have a catastrophic effect on the artist's soul. Too much rejection or criticism can cause artists to lose faith in their mission and/or talent, or give up on their passion. But it is not really rejection that can adversely affect artists; rather, it is how they react to rejection that is important. It is not the judgment of others that truly affects us, the problem occurs when we allow the rejection by others to cause us to feel negatively about ourselves—when we reject ourselves.

One must accept rejection as part of the process and move on when it occurs, just as death is a part of life. If we cannot manage rejection, feelings such as anger, frustration, bitterness, or cynicism can occupy the soul and destroy our careers. Personalizing rejection is dangerous. It is very hard for many of us not to personalize rejection, but it is bad for us when we do. When we fail to manage our responses to adversity, we can become involved with blame, seeing all our misfortune, including rejection, as the fault of others.

For some, the antidote to rejection can be to make more art; pain can be a motivator. For others, rejection can be difficult. In some cases, artists mix their self-image and their work—their self-*worth* and their work. Over time, their reaction to rejection can change. Whereas once rejection could be easily dismissed, cumulative rejection can lead to feelings of personal rejection, loss, withdrawal, and depression in sensitive artists.

Huge numbers of artists—performing, visual, literary, the whole lot of them—are rejected every day. Think about actors going to several auditions a day. Rejections occur for many reasons that have nothing to do with talent. Gatekeepers of exhibition spaces, juries, calls, et cetera, have mandates to fulfill that may require them to balance the gender or ethnicity of selected artists, or they may have to make selections to meet geographic objectives. Gatekeepers may have strong preferences, just as many artists do, that preclude the selection of your work. And there can be a compromise to neutral visual art programming due to the prejudices of board members, donors, and staff. Also, the artists' work may meet the standards of a gallery to which they submit, but the subject of the work, the style, or the media may render the artists ineligible due to the exhibition history of the gallery. (They have proposed a show of portraits, but the gallery has just recently had a portrait exhibition, for example.)

There can be a number of reasons for which you are rejected that have nothing to do with your skill and the value of your work. The key thing to remember when your work is rejected is that it is only your work that has been rejected, not you. And not even "your work," just the specific works that you submitted for consideration have, for one reason or another, been rejected.

If rejection leads to feelings of inadequacy, depression, or failure, you have several remedial options to consider. Any one of them, or any other healing exercise that you may prefer, will definitely work if, and only if, you sincerely want to regain your faith and drive. When rejected, it is helpful to recover by doing one or all of the following:

1. Recall past successes.
2. Pour your energy into applications to other venues or initiate a new project.
3. Set the rejection in context—ask yourself, "What is more important—this rejection or my friendships?"
4. Take self-help steps such as talking with peers and getting support or doing yoga or some other meditative practice.
5. Engage an artist friend as a coach and provide the same services to your friend.
6. Consider professional counseling.

And remember, some artists have established their careers from rejection. There is a strong tradition of the "salon des réfusés" in art. The most famous such salon was in response to the Paris Salon of 1863. The Paris Salon was an annual official exhibition of leading artists of the time. In 1863, the jury of the salon rejected 3,000 pieces, including Édouard Manet's Le Déjeuner sur l'herbe and James McNeill Whistler's *Girl in White*. The rejected artists mounted their own exhibition with the patronage of Emperor Napoleon III in an annex of the official salon, and the emerging avant-garde movement in art was introduced to the world. Also, the long and proud tradition of Artropolis exhibitions in Vancouver began as a salon des réfusés in reaction to the Vancouver Art Gallery's focus on too few artists (in the opinion of many local artists).

Finally, there is one good thing about rejection letters—a proven benefit! Save your rejection emails and letters in case you are ever audited. If you have annual losses declared in your income taxes as an artist, you face an increased risk of being audited by Revenue Canada, and if you are, your rejection letters can attest to both your professional ambitions and the reason for your losses.

Example: Vincent

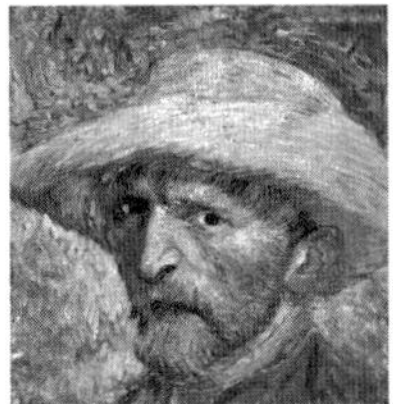

Vincent was a Dutch artist born in 1863. He was a teacher and missionary before he began painting when he was seventeen. His work was not popular at all; he failed to show it to any degree and sold only one piece while alive, even though he produced more than 2,000 works. But posthumously, he is credited as one of the founders of Expressionism and his work now regularly sells for millions. In 1990, his piece, *Portrait of Dr. Gachet,* sold at auction for $129.7 million US—the fourth highest price ever paid for a work of art.

Some Professional Observations

Linda Findlay is a Vancouver private psychology practitioner in Vancouver. She is also a practicing visual artist with a strong exhibition history. Findlay identifies creative blocks as her primary therapeutic concern. She says, "Creative blocks can lead to depression and low self-esteem, and that can perpetuate or extend the creative block."

The PhD thesis of Dr Geraldine Brooks is entitled "Creative Labours: The Lives and Careers of Women Artists." She is a registered psychologist in private practice in Vancouver. In her thesis, Brooks refers to themes of being an outsider (feeling alien, lonely, or misunderstood, outside of the norm), validation from external recognition, and obstruction (sexism, self-doubt).

Other themes identified by these therapists are the conflict between the needs of the artist versus the needs of others and the sense of a struggle to assume the identity of an artist. And there is also the issue of sensitivity.

"Many creative people have heightened sensitivity to the world around them," says Findlay. "This heightened awareness results in artists seeing many things in their families and the world around them that others do not see or do not want to admit to seeing. [They] often carry the burden of others." Brooks also has studied the issue of sensitivity: "So often the unique way creative people look at the world is pathologized—that is, their peers or family see sensitivity as a problem that needs to be fixed."

Brooks also points out that there are also positive themes such as the sense of independence and freedom that comes with the creative lifestyle, and the sense of connection and belonging through art. And when creative people suffer, some can channel their pain in positive ways, using pain as inspiration. (Remember Bob Geldof and the first rock concert benefiting famine relief in Ethiopia?) Other creative people may work out their feelings through their art, but some succumb to their depressions, and when this happens, counseling can be valuable. Therapeutic drugs, when appropriate, provide relief for some individuals seeking improved mental health.

Peer Communities

One very effective way to combat feelings of depression or sadness over rejections (and to advance your career) is to network with other artists. Peer networks function practically, but they also can be effective as a support group when one needs to talk through a crisis. There comes a tremendous sense of satisfaction when talking something out with the right someone—nothing beats the concurrence of someone who truly understands what you need to talk about.

Since an early point in Canadian history, artists have formed societies to advance themselves collectively and individually, both professionals and amateurs. Their membership and mandates reflect the general society; artists have grouped by age, faith, gender, aesthetic theory, media, and sexual preference. Artists have formed societies to lobby governments and their agencies, create group exhibitions, and/or and to create public venues such as artist-run centres. Throughout Canada, artists are organized and there is likely an artists' association to serve every artist. Certainly, there are far more urban resources than rural, but one way or another, in person or virtually, artists can enjoy peer assembly.

Some visual art communities that provide excellent professional development services for visual artists are listed below. They are relevant to all visual artists in Canada—except Malaspina Printmakers, which is an example of a valuable local resource for artists. The web, your local library, local art teachers, and arts councils can help you identify visual art communities closest to you, or you can do research online.

1. **CARFAC** is the acronym of Canadian Artists Representation/Le front des artists canadiens. As mentioned in previous chapters, CARFAC is Canada's national service organization for professional

artists. It has a long and proud history of serving visual artists in Canada, but a very large percentage of Canadians who self-identify as professional visual artists do not belong to CARFAC, so the effectiveness of the society as an advocacy organization is not as strong as it could or should be.

This is, however, a community that deserves your interest and support. The people involved with CARFAC are dedicated professionals who are working in your best interests everyday. In particular, the CARFAC Copyright Collective is something every professional visual artist should support. Find out about CARFAC and the collective at *carfac.ca*.

2. **The Federation of Canadian Artists (FCA)**: the FCA is a highly effective membership-driven association. It is active in supporting the professional development of members who belong to one of their professional association categories. Members are juried into associate status (members consistently having demonstrated superior ability in the general members' exhibitions and through other jury criteria) and senior status (artists are elected once a year by a consensus of twelve or more existing senior FCA members).

   The FCA runs a gallery on Granville Island in Vancouver and members also have regional shows. The FCA is an excellent example of a group of artists forming a group in which to network and advance their professional development. Learn more about the federation at *artists.ca*.

3. **My Art Club**: today, you have to consider the myriad of virtual communities available to you through websites, blogs, and chat groups. Artists living in an isolated area and who are comfortable with technology should visit *myartclub.com* if they are interested in establishing a presence on the web. This is a comprehensive web-based, professional-oriented service site for visual artists. You pay for the service, but the site provides excellent value for money. Being a virtual community, its services and benefits are available to you when you want them—there are no real-word community meetings. Belonging to this community can enhance your membership in the real-world community to which you belong.

4. **Malaspina Printmakers:** this group is an excellent model of a service organization that serves member artists needing special (and expensive) equipment. Joining the society gives members access to a very professional studio through a reasonable rental program. Printmakers who cannot afford to set up their own studio with all the equipment required for etching, screen printing, mezzotinting, engraving, lithography, et cetera, can effectively address their needs by becoming a member. The society also operates a gallery and provides sales and professional development services for its members. To learn more about Malaspina Printmakers, visit *malaspinaprintmakers.com*.
5. **Local & regional arts councils:** British Columbia has regional arts councils that each serve their communities organically to serve the unique needs of the local artists. In rural centres where there is not a sufficient density of artists to form a visual art organization, artists can work with local arts councils to create community by organizing annual shows, slide nights, and professional development seminars.

Other Community Resources

1. **Google:** *google.com* makes it easy to find resources. The more skilled you are at Internet searching, the more likely your time spent online will yield beneficial results. Learn from Google, friends, your local library, or a teacher on how to use quotation marks, identifying the right key words, and other tricks to narrow your searches.
2. **The Organization of Saskatchewan Arts Councils:** this organization acts as an umbrella for community arts councils and schools across the province. (Tel: 306-586-1250; fax: 306-586-1550; email: *info@osac.sk.ca*; website: osac.sk.ca)
3. **SaskCulture Inc.:** a community-driven, non-profit organization that works with members to build a culturally vibrant Saskatchewan. (Tel: 306-780-9284; fax: 306-780-9252; website: *saskculture.sk.ca*)
4. **The Manitoba Arts Network:** this organization supports the promotion and development of arts and culture in rural and remote Manitoba communities. (Tel: 204-943-0036; fax: 204-943-1126; email: info@communityarts.mb.ca; website: *communityarts.mb.ca*)

5. **Community Arts Ontario:** a network of arts agencies, institutions, and municipalities across Ontario as well as individual artists and public supporters. (Tel: 416-598-1128 or toll-free: 800-806-2302; fax: 416-598-4468; email: info@artsonline.ca; website: *artsonline.ca*)
6. **The Nova Scotia Cultural Network:** a not-for-profit society that promotes broad-based cultural development and indigenous cultural expression throughout the province. (Tel: 902-423-4456; fax: 902-423-4248; email: *network@culture.ns.ca*; website: culture.ns.ca)
7. **The Newfoundland and Labrador Arts Council:** a non-profit organization whose purpose is to foster the arts of the province by operating financial assistance programs, providing services and resources, and working with government and the community for development in the arts. (Tel: 709-726-2212; fax: 709-726-0619; email: nlacmail@newcomm.net; website: *nlac.nf.ca*)
8. **Nunavut Arts and Crafts Association:** the NACA is a non-profit incorporated society that promotes the growth and appreciation of Nunavut artists, and the production of their arts and crafts. (Tel: 867-979-7808; fax: 867-979-6880; email: *arts@nunanet.com*; website: *nacaarts.org*)

Estate Planning

Denial is a key strategic tool for human beings; we seem to be hardwired for denial. Perhaps nothing challenges acceptance more than death. Considerate people make it easy for their executors to do what they have to do. If your executor is a close friend or family member, they have to spring into action at a time when they may be feeling emotional pain over your loss, so making plans helps you, your executor, and your beneficiaries.

The complexities of good estate planning go far beyond just making a will. You should gather all the information your executor will need (e.g., bank account information, annotated inventories, a contact list for notification) and keep it in an identified place. There are memorial societies in Canada can provide you with guidance about preparations. Use Google to see if there is such an organization in or near your community. Also, consult with your tax advisor regarding options for your inventory of unsold works.

The Artist's Legacy

If you have ever seen TV program, *Antiques Roadshow*, you will know the importance of the provenance, or history, of an artwork. Even if it is only your family, future generations love to know the story of all works of art and objects of great financial or sentimental value. On *Antiques Roadshow*, one often sees items that were originally practical and manufactured by hand or machine. Their provenance often concerns the pieces' owners as opposed to their creators, but the artworks featured on the show, whenever possible, focus on the creator as well as its ownership. *Antiques Roadshow* reveals how important it is that the history of the artist, whenever possible, remains attached to an artwork—that is, after all, why the tradition of signing artworks began.

Dedicated amateur and professional artists often produce hundreds of pieces of art during the course of their careers. As the risk of death increases, artists are wise to make plans for their artwork (in particular terms) and not leave their work as part of their general estate.

The final and perhaps greatest value of having an inventory diary is at the time of your death; refer to it in your will. Keeping a detailed inventory of all your creations and prices is very valuable to your executor. Also, leave a record of your thoughts about key pieces or about themes in your work and a brief biography. Your story is part of your creative legacy.

Often, when an artist dies, she or he leaves behind unsold art. Unsigned work has to be "signed" posthumously in order to authenticate it. Sometimes, an estate stamp is made with a facsimile of the artist's signature and unsigned pieces are stamped. Otherwise, the art may be estate-stamped and also hand-signed by a qualified third party such as an executor; or a qualified third party may sign it with the artist's name instead of her or his own.

None of the above alternatives match the value of you signing all your work. Galleries and collectors regard unsigned or posthumously signed works of art as less significant or desirable than signed works of art. When they find themselves dealing with unsigned art (or art signed by someone other than the artist), they wonder why didn't the artist sign this piece—if the artist did not like this piece or thought of it as incomplete, did he or she consider it unworthy of a signature? Always sign your art.

If you keep an accurate professional inventory diary, your art will be well organized for your executor. You will have eliminated anyone from having to guess when particular works of art were made, where they belonged in relation to the rest of your art, or what they mean. A detailed inventory with notes will allow your executor to understand the continuity of your career through your art. (You may wish to appoint one executor for your estate and another for you artistic inventory and legacy.)

Price all your art when you enter it into inventory. Include current retail and/or wholesale prices if applicable. Seriously consider making an audio or audiovisual record of your career and leaving it for your executor. Even a relatively short piece can add immeasurably to your legacy as an artist.

Finally, have a disposition strategy. You, your executor, and your gallery should work together to establish a sales strategy for any remaining inventory at the time of your death (or if you become intestate). Not having a plan can mean your work may be sold randomly and without exclusivity, offered to anyone the executor or gallery knows, offered at arbitrary prices, or dumped onto the market all at once. An estate without such a plan will not serve any artist well.

Have, in essence, a post-mortem marketing plan for your executor(s) to follow:

1. Provide your executor with complete contact information for your gallery and all your professional representatives, along with instructions on how to work with these people. By planning ahead and sharing your strategy with all concerned parties, they will have the chance to clearly understand your plan and better be able to execute it.
2. Leave clear instructions on how your art is to be divided among family members, institutions, galleries, and other relevant parties. Make sure that everyone understands what they are going to get and, if necessary, why they are getting it.
3. Depending on the size of inventory *intended for the market* remaining unsold at the time of your death, leave a disposition plan that clearly lays out the volume and pace at which your inventory will be shown and/or sold.
4. All instructions should be clear and sufficiently detailed in order to prevent infighting, arguments, or legal disputes over who owns or controls what, and how much the art is worth.

15

Conservation & Framing

"There's no retirement for an artist, it's your way of living so there's no end to it." —*Henry Moore*

"There is a precedent in Canadian case law that requires visual artists to know and declare the 'shelf-life' of the work they create." —*C. T.*

Conservation

In the 1990s, an artist was commissioned to create a painting for a couple in Toronto who had just built a new home. The couple invited the artist to their home so he could see where the work was to hang and to discuss the desired colour palette before he began painting. The artist completed the work and it was installed. Several years later, the pigment in some of the paint used faded dramatically, so the homeowners successfully sued the artist for damages. The judge in the case ruled that artists have a responsibility to make work that will last (or to declare its probable lifespan).

Artists creating work for sale must evaluate the permanence of the materials they use and pay attention, therefore, to how their artwork is stored, shown, and transported (by them and by any galleries with whom they work).

Choosing Materials

Using "archival quality" or "museum quality" materials that have guarantees of permanence preserves your work and the investment of your collectors: the quality of the materials you use speaks to your professionalism. It is not just the substrates and the pigments in your media that are important, the use of thinners, solvents, glues, and other additives also must be considered. Not only is using materials that will last important, advertising your use of these materials is a valuable and clever marketing practice. Labeling your work as "conservationally sound" gives buyers confidence in your work and in you. If, beyond that, you offer customers information on the hanging and storing of your art, you will stand out and may enjoy repeat business. By thinking of the buyers, you greatly enhance their sales experience.

The Enemies of Art

To make, store, and exhibit your work safely, you must know your enemies. They are you (the artist), ultraviolet light, pollution, humidity, extreme temperature, temperature variance, insects, and molds.

The Artist

Man and nature are the enemies of art. Not unsurprisingly, you are the greatest threat to your artwork—whether you made or bought it. (Consider

Steve Wynn's elbow puncturing his $48 million painting *Le Rêve* or Picasso's 1932 portrait of his mistress, Marie-ThérPse Walter.) Most of the damage done to contemporary art is by accident by artists in their studios. How you move work is important, as are how and where you store it.

Light

The visible spectrum consists of the colors perceivable by the human eye (wavelengths ranging from about 400 nanometres [violet] to about 700 nanometres [red]). You can see this spectrum when a beam of sunlight passes through a prism to form a rainbow of colour. The radiation refracted by the prism actually extends farther in both directions to ultraviolet (UV) light that cannot be perceived by the human eye. UV light is divided into three regions:

1. The near regions: 350–380 nanometres and used in fluorescence.
2. The far regions: 200–300 nanometres and used in sunlamps, sterilizing lamps, full-spectrum botanical lamps.
3. The vacuum regions: under 200 nanometres—the final wavelengths that cause the greatest damage and are the ones screened by the Earth's ozone layer.

Direct UV light—even worse, UV light reflected off snow, glass, or water—is the most significant non-human enemy of art. It is the greatest cause of damage to completed artwork. Natural light is the dominant source of UV light; fluorescent tubes, energy-saving compact fluorescent lamps, and discharge lamps produce considerable UV light. Incandescent lamps, reflector spot lamps and lamps with directional or spotting fittings produce less UV than natural or fluorescent light, but they can cause damage to artwork; LED and fibre-optic light produce barely any UV light.

Pollution

Artists must be concerned about unwanted molecules of toxins that can be in their art materials or in the atmosphere in which the art is made or stored. Our atmosphere is increasingly toxic; consequently, conservation knowledge, materials, and practices are essential.

The fats and oils released into the atmosphere from the cooking of foods can contribute to the deterioration of artworks. Fat molecules cling to surfaces and penetrate substrates, allowing atmospheric pollutants to bind to the art; their presence also enhances the appeal of insects when fat molecules permeate substrates. Also, smoke from smoking materials, candles and fireplaces can create a tar film on the surface of art with chemicals that can damage art.

Moisture

When atmospheric pollutants (particularly sulphur dioxide which is a byproduct of the combustion of fossil fuels) form to create a water droplet, the droplet (rain) is acidic. Acid rain is eating architectural decoration around the world and it can be formed in artists' homes and in poorly constructed and/or sealed frames. This is a molecular-level danger that artists often do not consider: pollutants + humidity = acid. Moisture also facilitates the growth of molds.

Insects

The predominant insects of concern are silverfish, termites, book lice, cockroaches, and woodworms. They are attracted to the cellulose fibres of substrates, the sizing of papers (the agent in paper that retards absorption), and glues in frames and/or hinging materials.

Temperature

There are two concerns about temperature—degree and variance. Extreme temperatures are, of course, to be avoided. The heat radiating from (and rising from) fireplaces can create very warm conditions in a frame—particularly if the artwork is in a dark palette; high temperature due to the presence of ducts, appliances, and sunlight is also dangerous. Artwork should be hung and stored away from the cold air below all windows (particularly ones that open) and by doors.

Worse than extreme temperature, however, is temperature variance—the cycles of day and night and the variance produced by daytime and evening thermostat settings in your home, plus the seasonal cycles, create expansion/contraction tensions that can destroy both artwork and its frames. Even opening and closing windows in rooms hosting artwork can create a variance that produces structural tension. Temperature variance can also produce condensation in sealed and/or tightly fitting frames.

Handle with Care

For works of art on paper, the best way to protect art is to mat it as you make it and handle it as infrequently as possible. To prevent depositing oils and salts from your hands to the paper, it is advisable to wear cotton gloves. To move your artwork, slide a stiff paper or matboard below it before lifting it. Avoid eating, drinking, or smoking near the paper and keep pens, fluids, and markers at a distance. Here are other guidelines to help you protect your work:

1. Use archival hinging materials to hinge mats for works of art of value. Do not hinge your work with paper glue, rubber cement, pressure-sensitive tape, and/or masking tape. Paper clips leave rust marks and adhesives leave residue on surfaces that attract dirt and grime.
2. Do not touch the painting and frame surfaces with any cleaning solutions, cleaning cloths, sponges, feather dusters, vacuum brushes, or hand-held vacuum cleaners. If dust becomes a problem, a light dusting may be carried out with a soft badger or sable brush or with compressed air.
3. Do not use aerosols, sprays, insecticides, or oil-based pesticides near a painting.
4. Carry paintings by supporting the bottom and one side of the frame.
5. Avoid touching the front or backs of paintings.
6. Avoid storing your works of art on paper in basements or attics where temperatures and humidity levels fluctuate. Archival-quality matting, framing, and protective enclosures will protect works on paper from environmental toxins, moisture and physical damage.
7. Pastels, graphite and work in conté crayon require particular care. These materials have a relatively weak bond with their substrate and must be matted for storage (with a four-ply or more top mat). Matted works in these fibrous media should also be framed or stored in archival boxes to prevent damage.

Some artworks utilize materials that, due to their chemical composition, are inherently unstable and will degrade rapidly. Conservators refer to this as “inherent vice” in an artwork. Wood-based papers and iron gall ink are two examples of materials with this built-in capacity to self-destruct; artists should advise buyers of work of such compromised integrity. Wood-pulp paper forms acidic compounds that break down paper fibres. Iron gall ink is made from oak galls and ferrous sulphate that, over time, emits sulphuric acid and destroys the paper on which the ink is printed. Storage or display in low temperature and relative humidity may reduce the rate of degradation.

Measuring & Controlling Light

The easiest way to measure reflected light intensity is with a camera light meter. The Canadian Conservation Institute suggests using a 35mm single lens reflex camera with a built-in light meter, and a twelve- by sixteen-inch white card.

1. Set the camera film-speed reading at 800 ASA, and set the shutter speed at 1/60 of a second.
2. Have someone hold the white card in front of the artwork and at the same angle as the work.
3. Position the camera so that the card just fills the view screen.
4. Adjust the aperture setting until the camera's:
   f4 indicates 50 lux or 4.6 footcandles
   f5.6 indicates100 lux or 9.3 footcandles
   f8 indicates 200 lux or 18.6 footcandles
   f11 indicates 400 lux or 37.2 footcandles

There is an axiom that balances light levels with exposure time. If lighting is limited to an eight-hour day, using this measuring method produces results to within three footcandles of a professional footcandle meter reading, and once you know the intensity level of the lighting in your home, studio, and/or gallery, you can follow the following guidelines:

1. For works on paper and sensitive materials, such as prints, drawings, watercolors, dyed fabrics, and manuscripts, exposure should be limited to 50 lux (5–10-footcandles).
2. For oil paintings, acrylics, watercolours, most photographs, ivory, and work containing or finished with organic materials such as resins, waxes and varnishes, exposure should be limited to 150 lux (15-footcandles).

To put things simply, avoid hanging your artwork where it may be exposed to direct or reflected sunlight through windows and skylights. Use curtains, blinds, or shutters in rooms where you hang your artwork and close them when the room is empty. Consider framing art behind glazing material (glass or plastic) that filters ultraviolet light, and store you work in a dark environment that is also dust-free, at a constant temperature and, ideally, with controlled humidity.

Controlling Moisture, Insects & Pollutants

First, know your climate. Learn the weather rhythms of your area: understand the characteristics of your seasons. How humid is it in summer and winter? Are there extremes of humidity through the year? What are the seasonal temperature variances? Next, know your environment(s). How do you heat your house/studio? In what direction are windows in your art-making, storage, and display locations oriented? Do they admit direct light? Reflected light? Are the windows of these areas light reflective? Study the long-term environments of your artworks and consider humidifiers, UV filtering films, air purifiers, and your heating and cooling practices for these environments as necessary. Fumigate if your environmental analysis reveals the presence of insects.

The best protection against moisture and pollutants is proper storage of completed work—particularly with works on paper. Paper is so vulnerable. Archival boxes and portfolios are worth the investment if you maintain inventory over time. Archival boxes effectively protect artwork that is neither matted nor framed. An even better storage strategy for works of art on paper is archival matting followed by storage in a safe environment such as conservation locker or archival box or frame. Silicate sacs can add protection in particularly humid climates.

Yes, there is a cost to following sound conservational practices, but there is more to your return on the investment than permanence, safety, and peace of mind. When you follow sound conservational practices, curators, gallery owners, and buyers or potential buyers will see that you respect your work and believe in its value. Your investment in conservation speaks to your professionalism.

Framing Works of Art on Paper

The shape, finish, and colour of the molding you choose for your frame is a subjective decision, as are many of the decisions about your matboard: its colour, thickness, texture, width, and core colour. Other subjective decisions about matting include whether to use a single, double, or triple mat, the shape of the mat window, and whether or not the edges of the substrate (paper bearing the image) is visible ("floating") or not.

From a business and marketing perspective, a discussion of framing is important because frames protect your work, enhance the presentation of your art, and are an added value that increase your per-sales net profit, and frames and mats come in standard sizes and creating work that fits in standard sizes saves you money.

A few simple tips about frames and mats are:

1. Neutral mats and simple, clean frame moldings are best for works being offered for sale—the purpose of using mats is to isolate the image from the distractions of the rest of the viewer's vision; by surrounding the art with a neutral band, the image is better presented.
2. Dark-coloured frames with (warm) white mats are a standard in gallery practices.
3. The mat and frame are about showcasing the art, not matching room décor.

And finally, good framing involves:

1. Choosing the right mat and frame dimensions.
2. Choosing the right frame molding (one that provides a tight seal).
3. Selecting the right matting colour and the right matting weight (ply).
4. Choosing the best hinging materials (in terms of quality and strength).
5. Choosing the right glazing materials (glass, Plexiglas, UV-filtered glazing).
6. Sealing the frame.
7. Ensuring good airflow around the frame.

Matting Artwork

When you are matting an image on paper, there are generally two mats: the top mat and the back mat. These mats sandwich your art in a safe envelope within the frame. There may be more than one top mat; framing choices are easily researched with your art-supply or framing store or online.

The top mat usually covers the substrate paper completely; the mat window (the hole cut in the top mat to reveal the artwork beneath) is cut into the top mat to reveal only your image. When this is done, the window should be

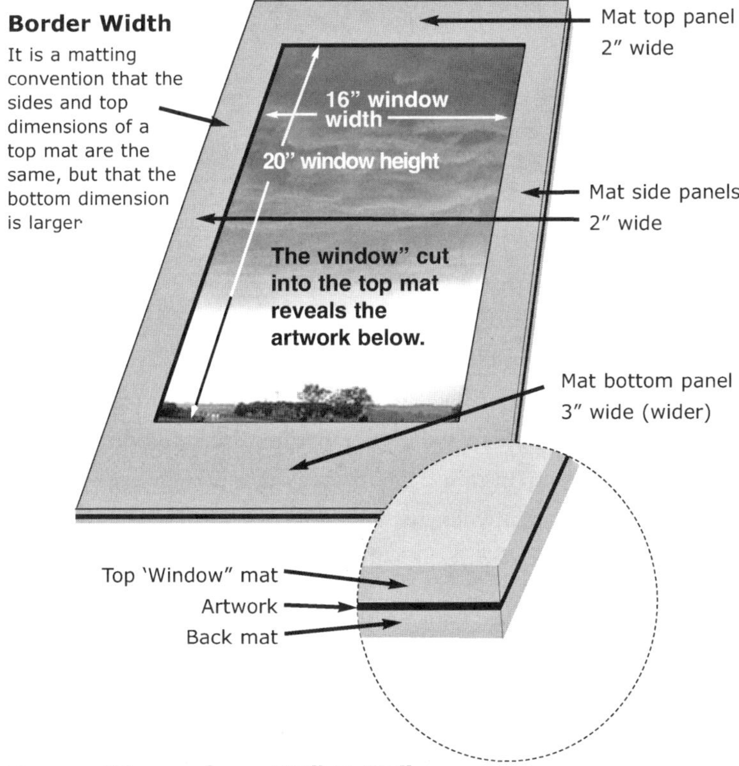

Frame Dimensions 20″ X 25″

Frame Width = side panel width + window width + side panel width.
The frame for this mat will be 20″ wide (2″ + 16″ + 2″ = 20″).

Frame Height = top panel width + window height + bottom panel width.
The frame for this mat will be 20″ high (2″ + 20″ + 3″ = 25″).

Figure 15.1. Sample mat and frame dimensions

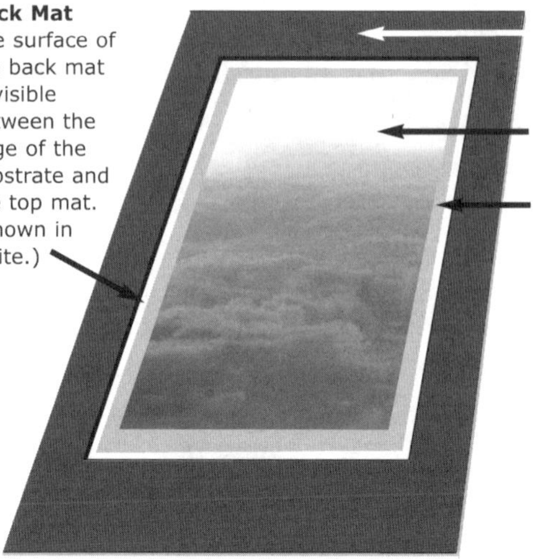

Figure 15.2. A floating image

cut to dimensions a 1/2-inch smaller than the image size in both directions. For example, an image that is 11 by 16 inches should have a window in the top mat that is 10.5 by 15.5 inches. The top mat will then conceal a 1/4-inch of the image all round, giving the image a nice clean edge in the frame.

When you "float" an image, the top mat surrounds and reveals both the image *and* the substrate to its edges. In this case, the window is cut to dimensions a 1/4-inch (or more) larger than the substrate size in both directions so that the top mat will leave a 1/2-inch (or more) view of the surface of the back mat surrounding the floated substrate. When floating your image, it is important to choose a surface for your back mat will enhance the presentation of your work because it will be seen.

The outside dimensions of your mat equal your frame size. If your window is 6 inches wide and the side panels of your mat are 2 inches each, your mat is 10 inches wide; if the window height is 10 inches and the top mat panel is 2 inches and the bottom is 3 inches the mat height is 15 inches. The frame for this matted work will therefore be 10 by 15 inches.

Signature/Edition Information

When you are framing prints bearing a signature, an edition number, and/or name, you want have this information seen by viewers. This window

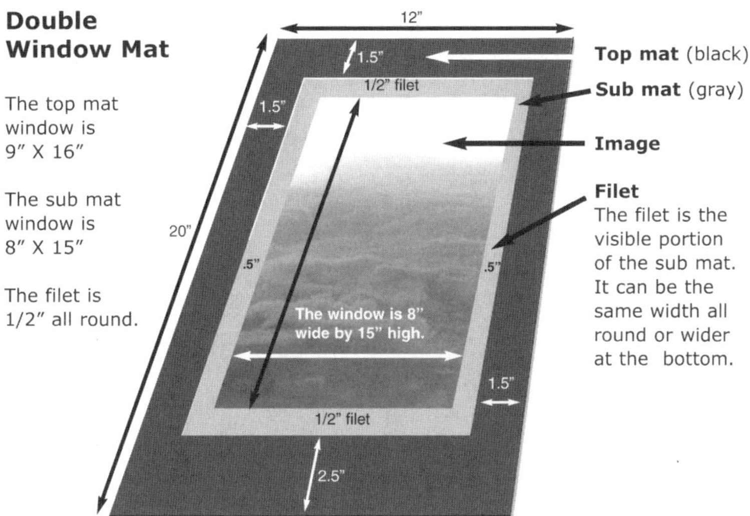

Figure 15.3. Double window mat

you cut in your top mat must be measured and cut so as to reveal this information.

The Back Mat

The back mat provides strength and stability. The top surface is important if you are floating an image in the frame (because it will form a border around the floating work). Otherwise, it is an invisible component of the mat once a work is framed. However, because the substrate is attached to the back mat, it is the most important mat to consider in terms of its quality. The entire substrate rests against the back mat, so if it contains contaminants, they can leach into your substrate.

Matboard Quality

Nomenclature describing matboard quality varies in different areas, but framers generally work with three levels of matboard quality. This primer will use the terms "museum," "conservation," and "regular" to describe matboard levels. Museum-quality matboards are made of cotton linter or rag fibres; the other levels are often made of wood pulp fibres—sometimes with a surface layer of cotton linter or rag fibre paper.

1. Museum: acid-free, all cotton fibre, and conservationally sound,

museum-quality matboard provides the greatest degree of protection for your artwork. Museum-quality matboard is available in predominantly white (warm and cool), off-white and black.

2. Conservation: similar to museum board, but conservation-quality matboard is made of purified, acid-free wood pulp with high alpha cellulose content. Coloured conservation boards combine a colour layer fused to a cotton fibre or pure cellulose core.
3. Regular: usually made of wood pulp buffered with calcium carbonate for stabilization, regular-quality matboards come in a wide range of colours and are economical.

The best mats for artwork destined for showing and selling are off-white, warm white, or a cream-coloured mat that is of conservation or museum quality. A cool white mat or pure white mat can make the work's whites look muddy or dirty. Similarly, a pure black mat can make blacks in it look grey. Coloured mats should be avoided in work for the marketplace.

If you choose to use a coloured mat, only use a colour in the composition and use a shade of the colour in the composition (not the actual colour) or you will lessen the impact of the colour in the composition.

Mat Thickness (Ply)

The purpose of top mats is to protect the artwork from touching the glazing material as well as to enhance the presentation of the composition. The top mat must be thick enough to protect the work, but not so thick as to leave too much space between the art and the glass or Plexiglas. Artwork with texture or depth (done, for example, in a fibrous medium such as conté crayon or pastel) should use three- or four-ply for the top mat (or two, two-ply top mats). Using top mats that are too thick can lead to problems: if the composition is dark, condensation can form in the frame.

Attaching Artwork to a Mat (Hinging)

Hinging is the name given to the method of fastening artwork to its back mat and to the method of attaching the top mat to the back mat. Using glues, tapes, and any other fastening methods are inappropriate. Hinges are made of archival paper that expands and contracts with temperature and humidity,

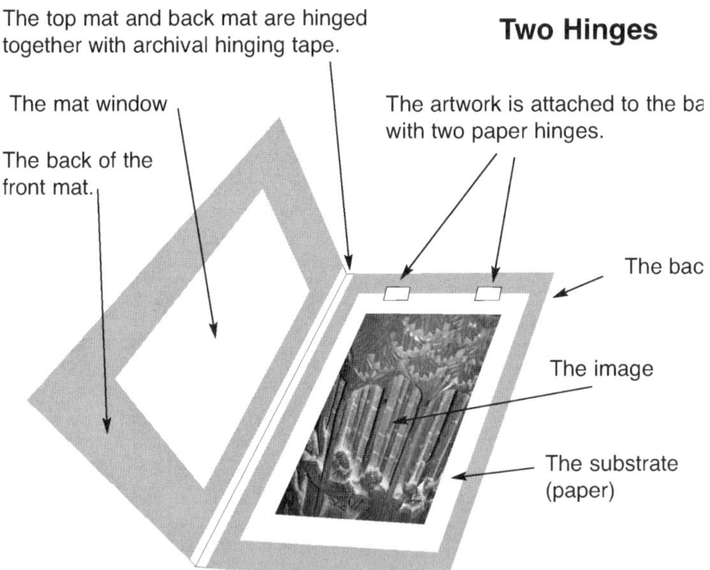

Figure 15.4. Two hinges

just as the substrate of your artwork does. Hinges prevent buckling; they are designed to be weaker than the paper to which they are attached so that should the frame drop, the artwork will tear away from the back mat, reducing the risk of damage to the piece.

The front (window) mat and the back mat should be hinged together (vertically or horizontally) first. Use an acid-free hinging tape to attach your mats together either vertically or horizontally. Both mats of the same dimension should fit snugly into their frame. The simplest hinge is shown in the diagram in figure 15.4: two paper hinges attach the substrate to the back mat in the diagram in a way that allows the image to be seen clearly and cleanly through the window of the top mat when the mat is closed and the hinges are concealed.

When you are hinging a paper substrate to a back mat, do not use too many or hinges that are too large. Doing so is counter-productive; the idea is to lightly hold the substrate in place so that the image is clearly visible but able to "breathe." When you are matting a heavy substrate, archival cloth tape can be used in this way instead of paper hinges. For large works on paper, reinforced hinges are better. Floating images are attached with either a reinforced "V" or "S" hinge.

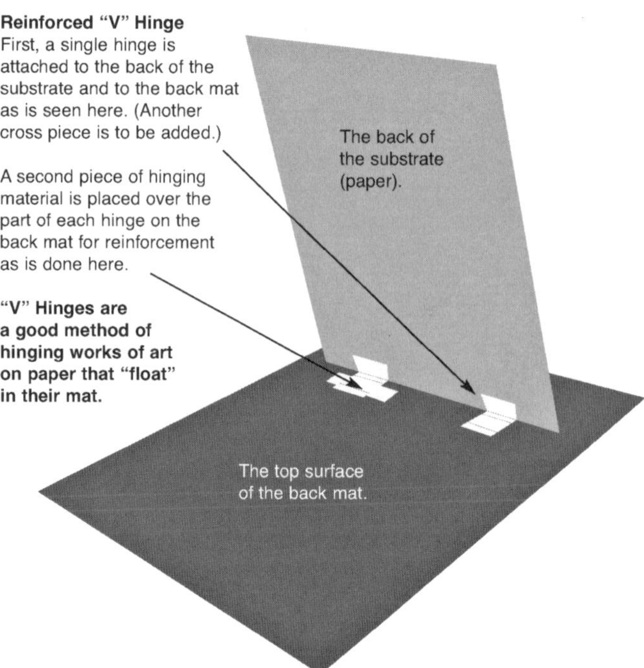

Figure 15.5. The reinforced "V" hinge

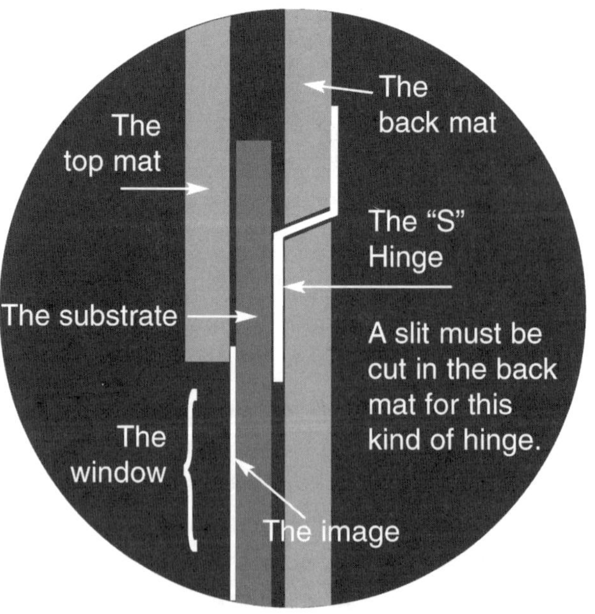

Figure 15.6. The "S" hinge

Sealing & Bumpers

If you are framing a work of art (on paper) to museum or conservation standards, you will want to seal the back of the frame with gummed paper or archival tape. Tape all four sides of the back of the frame where the backing material meets the frame molding to ensure your artwork is protected in its frame. The frame should be opened, the glazing cleaned, and the frame re-sealed with new tape every five years.

Bumpers are very small self-adhesive rubber or wooden "buttons" that are stuck onto the back two lower corners (or all four corners) of the frame. Bumpers hold the frame away from the wall on which they are hung, allowing air to circulate around the frame. This is particularly important if the wall on which the art is hanging contains hot or cold plumbing or hosts a heat source.

Framing Paintings on Stretched Canvas

There is a range of opinion on the framing of stretched canvas—far too great a range to deal with at length in this primer. Works on canvas are often hung without frames and it is not a problem for many buyers to purchase canvases without frames; doing so allows them to frame, if desired, to their own taste and conventions. Some artists feel showing and selling works on canvas unframed focuses the viewers' eyes on the work.

Works on canvas should, however, be hung for storage as well as display. Hanging a work, keeps it out of danger in your studio if you do not have access to a proper canvas storage facility. Hanging a work by its stretcher is reasonable for a certain period of time, but the stretcher, if not well assembled, can weaken over time and then a frame will be required to keep the integrity of the piece (or it may have to be re-stretched). If, on the edges of your work, potential buyers can see fastening devices and dribbles of paint, some kind of framing is advisable—or paint or otherwise tidy up the edge.

Here are some points to consider when framing canvases (artists are advised to follow conventions or their own instinct when it comes to framing work done on stretched canvas):

1. The more visible the frame, the less focus on the art.
2. Using wood frames is a popular convention in the framing of canvas.

3. Small paintings that are strong can be reinforced with a large frame and command a large expanse of wall.
4. Medium- to large-sized contemporary art shows well with minimalist approach; a narrow floating frame can dramatically present a piece (3/8 to 1/2 inch).
5. Choose too thin over too thick.
6. Remember, the frame is background—a safe bet, especially for a piece being sold, is a simple molding with a subtle finish.
7. Consult with, or use, the services of a framing professional.

APPENDIX A

CARFAC Ontario Advisory Notes

CARFAC Ontario
Canadian Artists' Representation/Le front des artistes canadiens
401 Richmond Street West, Suite 440,
Toronto, Ontario, M5V 3A8
t: 416-340-8850/1-877-890-8850
f: 416-340-7653
www.carfacontario.ca
Email: via "Contact" on their website

The CARFAC Ontario Advisory Notes are brief documents (from 3 to 17 pages long) that summarize everything you need to know on a specific topic relating to your artistic practice. These are available on a CD-ROM in PDF format at:

www.carfacontario.ca/services/advisory_notes

The CD includes articles on the following topics:

1. Dealer Checklist Artist
2. Exhibition Checklist
3. Artist Groups: Community Development for Artists
4. Artist/Mural Checklist
5. Sample Artist/Mural Contract - Notes
6. Artist/Public Gallery Exhibition Agreement
7. Business Entities for Artists
8. Certificate of Canadian Origin
9. Copyright & Commissioned Works
10. Copyright for Visual Artists
11. Exhibiting/Selling Outside of Canada

12. GST & Artists
13. Guidelines for Organizing Art Commission Competitions
14. Guidelines for Professional Standards in the Organization of Juried Exhibitions
15. Guidelines for Professional Standards in the Organization of Fund-raising Events
16. Health Hazards & Safety Tips for Artists
17. Hidden Dangers in the Sale of Artworks
18. Insuring Your Artwork
19. Marketing Strategies for Visual Artists
20. Model Releases
21. Notes on Art in Public Places
22. Original Prints & Reproductions
23. Preparing for Your Tax Return
24. Re-transmission Rights
25. Trademarks & Trade Names
26. Using Photographic Images as Source Material
27. Warehouse Studio Health & Safety
28. Writing for Visual Artists

APPENDIX B

Sample Consignment and Sale Agreement Clauses

This agreement is entered into this ______day of ____________,

20___, by and between __________________ referred to herein as

"Dealer" and the individual named below referred to herein as "Artist."

Artist's name: ____

Artist's address: ______________________________________

Phone(s): ____

E-Mail: ____

Website(s): ____

Dealer's name: ____

Retail outlet's name: ___________________________________

Dealer's address: ______________________________________

Phone(s): ____

E-Mail: ____

Website(s): ____

Sample contract clauses

1 The artist agrees to provide the dealer with the quantity of artwork agreed to in their discussions. The work will be framed and in good condition; an artist's statement will be provided as well as a full professional resume.

2 The artist guarantees that the artwork(s) provided to the dealer are the original creations of the artist; the artist hold all rights and copyrights attached to each artwork listed in Appendix A of this agreement; all descriptions and information provided about the artist and the artwork(s) are true and accurate. The artist agrees is responsible for any and all costs and expenses (including reasonable attorney's fees) involved with any claims made that the artwork(s) is not an original creation of the artist or infringes upon a third-party's copyright.

3 The artist retains all rights to the reproduction of the artwork(s). However, the artist permits reproduction of the following piece(s) for publicity purposes involved with the exhibition and sale of consigned artwork.

____

____

____

4 The artist agrees to be a partner to the dealer in planning and executing advertising, merchandising and publicity involved with the exhibition and sale of the artist's work.

5 The artist assumes all costs involved with packing, shipping and insurance, liability and all other handling expenses incurred in the delivery of the artwork(s) to the dealer.

6 The dealer accepts the consignment inventory listed in Appendix A of this agreement.

7 Any additional artworks by the artist placed on consignment with the dealer will be covered by the terms of this agreement and listed on a separate appendix bearing the signatures of all signatories to this agreement.

8 The dealer may display, distribute, exhibit and sell the artist's work(s) of art but the artwork(s) shall not use the artwork for any other purpose without express consent in writing by the artist.

9 The artwork consigned for exhibition and sales will be numbered, signed described and priced at wholesale prices (based on your price rationale). The artworks covered by this contract are attached as Schedule A of this agreement.

10 The wholesale price of each artwork listed in Appendix A will be paid to the artist within 30 days of its sale.

11 The signatories to this agreement agree to meet and discuss their agreement in 60 days. If either party wishes to terminate the agreement at the meeting, all art shall be returned to the artist at the dealers expense (or held for pickup by the artist) and full payment for any sales will be made within 10 working days.

12 If both parties wish to maintain the agreement after the 60-day review, this agreement shall bind the parties for one year from the date this contract is signed.

13 The parties to this agreement will discuss renewal or an extension 30 days before this agreement is to expire.

14 Either party to this agreement can terminate their involvement by providing all other parties to the agreement with written notice to

terminate the agreement giving 30 days notice. If the agreement is terminated, all art shall be returned to the artist at the dealers expense (or held for pickup by the artist) and full payment for any sales will be made within 10 working days.

15 The dealer agrees to work to the best of his/her ability to sell as many of the artworks by the artist as is possible.

16 The dealer agrees to pay all promotion, advertising and exhibition costs. In the case of "third party" exhibitions, the artist and dealer will work to terms set out in a written agreement they shall undertake.

17 The dealer agrees to properly label and identify all exhibited artwork with the artist's name, the work's title, media used and any related information deemed appropriate by the artist or dealer.

18 It is the dealer's decision how many and how artworks will be displayed in the sale/exhibition space.

19 The dealer is responsible for all packing, shipping, insurance, liability and handling expenses involved with returning artwork to the artist, to buyers of the work and/or to any other sale/exhibition spaces negotiated by the dealer as agreed to by the artist.

20 The dealer is permitted to allow potential buyers to have possession of an artwork for 10 days on a sale-on-approval basis provided that the artist is informed in writing.

21 The dealer agrees to pay to the artist the wholesale price of an artwork (as listed in appendix A) within 30 days of the sale of the artwork.

22 The dealer and artist agree to the retail prices for the consigned pieces listed in appendix B. The dealer further agrees that any changes in prices will be agreed to in writing.

23 The dealer agrees to safely display and store the artwork and to insure them against theft, loss or damage. The dealer and his insurance agent agree to pay to the artist the wholesale prices listed in appendix A for any works lost or stolen.

24 The artist agrees that the dealer is not responsible or liable for the loss or damage to artwork(s) that results from natural disasters.

25 If the artist dies during the life of this agreement, the artist's executor will have the right to terminate the agreement under the terms outlined for dissolution of the agreement outlined in clauses # __________ of this agreement.

26 The dealer agrees to provide a annual statement to the artist on the one year anniversary of this agreement or on termination of the agreement. It will list:

A. Works sold:
- The title of the work sold
- The date of sale
- The sale price
- The name and contact information of the buyer
- Date of payment to artist

B. Works unsold being returned

27 All communication required in writing and relating to the relationship between the signatories shall be sent to the addresses listed in this agreement. Both parties agree to inform all signatories of any change in their contact information.

28 This agreement and its signed amendments or additions shall constitute the entire understanding between the signatories.

Finally, there should be a clause that identifies the governing laws in case there is litigation between the signatories to the agreement such as: "The signatories to this agreement recognize that the agreement is governed by the federal laws of Canada and (your province)."

The agreement should end with all signatories signing and dating the contract in space provided. Some lawyers suggest that each party to the agreement also initial and date each page. The agreement should also provide for a witness' signature and contact information.

APPENDIX C

Notes On Slides (Transparencies)

Slides are seldom used any more, but they still have a purpose in that they afford a better representation of colour than can digital images. Whereas most galleries now prefer digital images, several artists still require slides be taken for illustrative purposes and for secondary interviews with galleries—particularly the elite galleries.

1. Have all your slides taken in a professional studio with appropriate lighting and focus. Have a plain background if the image does not bleed to the edges of the slide.
2. Always read the requirements of any competition, gallery or call to which you are submitting slides to ensure you follow all directions. (Their directions may be different than guidelines provided here.)
3. Send copies; do not send original slides.
4. If part of your slide is to be masked, use professional photographic silver tape.
5. Use plastic slide mounts (cardboard mounts deteriorate). Damaged slides clog the carousel.
6. CLEARLY mount your name, the title, medium, date completed, and dimensions on the slide, attaching this information securely. If you print this information with self-adhesive paper to add to the slide, always check adhesion before submitting the slide. Adhesives loosen in the heat of the projectors and can come off. Put this information on the "front" of the slide.
7. When providing dimensions place an "H" in brackets after the height and a "W" in brackets with the width dimension. (Example: 50cm [W] X 31 cm [H].)
8. Place a red dot on the top left of the "front" of each slide-the "front" being the slide held as you would to view it in the light and explain the positioning of your dot in your cover letter. It is

important to know the top of the slide as well; the dot makes this clear.

9. Number your slides. Should you wish to have your slides viewed in a specific order, say so in your cover letter and number the slides in sequential order for the viewer.
10. Use a plastic slide sheet and insert all yours slides with information viewable on the same side. Put your name and contact information on the slide sheet.
11. Annotation: Provide text, permitted, on each slide and your purpose in providing it. Tell viewers what you want them to see in your slides IF THIS IS PERMITTED in the call or submission you are making. Ensure that the title of your work and the slide number correlate the descriptions to the correct slides.

APPENDIX D

Notes on Digital Images

File Formats

- Files are usually requested to be 72 ppi/dpi in resolution.
- The preferred compression format is "jpeg."
- The average preferred size of images is 900 pixels high by 1200 pixels wide.
- File size is important—no file should exceed 5 megabytes and files as large as 500 megabytes should not be bunched in a single email.

Labeling

- Number your images in the order in which you would like them viewed.
- If, for example, a gallery limits artists to ten illustrative digital images, label each one with a number (01 to 10) followed by your surname. Mary Cambell's images would be labeled as follows: 01Campbell.jpeg; 02Campbell.jpeg etc.
- Include a "Digital Image Description Sheet" with your submission on which you describe each work, linking each image to its appropriate description using the file names (01Campbell.jpeg; 02Campbell.jpeg, etc.). And, be sure to include your name and contact information on the "Description" sheet.
- CLEARLY list the title, medium, date completed, and dimensions of each work in its description. When providing dimensions place an "H" in brackets after the height and a "W" in brackets with the width dimension. (Example: 50cm [W] X 31 cm [H].) Depth (D) can be indicated as well if appropriate.
- Explanatory text, if necessary, should be limited to one sentence. (Your Artist Statement is the place for a more detailed accounting of your artistic purpose.)

- "Thmbnail" images are often helpful on your Description Sheet.
- Provide the images on a CD or DVD (and only the images on your sheet) and put your name and contact information on the disk.

Presentation Materials

- A CD-ROM in a case to prevent scratching.
- A DVD is an option, also protected in a case.
- If mailing a CD or DVD, be sure to mark your mailing envelope as "FRAGILE."

Choosing Representative Images

- Try to view the images you choose on a digital projector to ensure that your slides are of excellent quality. Correct any with problems.
- Choose images that are appropriate—that are truly representative of your work.
- A strong presentation sees all the images selected working together as a whole. In medium, style, subject and content, your images should be complimentary.
- If a background is visible in your images, ensure that it is clean and neutral.

APPENDIX E

Sample Media Release

(All names and contact information is fictitious.)

———— MEDIA RELEASE ————

(Release Date)
Vancouver, BC
FOR IMMEDIATE RELEASE

Contact: Cindy Chappell
Imagination Gallery
604-555-5555
artpublicists@gmail.com

DELIA BURNHAM IS CURING HER CANCER

Delia Burnham is curing her non-Hodgkin's lymphoma and she wants to show you how. She is curing herself with the help of my doctors and treatments, but most of all by visualizing the fight in her body between the chemicals and the lymphocytes that cause her disease. She sees the battles in her mind; her doctors see her battles won on her charts.

She has painted her cellular battles. She sees the fighting vividly during her treatments and in her one-person exhibition, *Chemical Landscapes*, she shows us what she sees as the chemicals sweep through her veins. "I see my cancer cells, my white blood cells, my T4 immune cells and the miracle chemicals that flow from IV tube to the battle front in my body," she says.

> *"If every patient had the positive attitude that Delia has! She is the most optimistic and determines patient I have ever seen."* — Dr. deVries

This is a celebratory exhibition. Come see how, in vibrant acrylics, the colours of her biochemistry and the contours of her interior landscapes are revealed. This is *not* an exhibition of anatomical or medical details; it is a revelation of the role of the spirit in healing.

"Delia's works are beautiful abstractions. The poignancy of her story adds impact to this powerful exhibition, but the works stand alone as beautiful landscapes. *—Gallery Director*

Delia Burnham's exhibition, "*Chemical Landscapes,*" opens Wednesday, April 16th 2008, 5:00 pm to 9:00 pm at the Imagination Gallery, 555 Granville Street, Vancouver. Ms. Burnham and Dr. deVries will be in attendance at the opening and for a special evening presentation entitled *Healing and the Arts*, on Wednesday April 23rd. The exhibition runs until Sunday May 18th; the gallery is open Wednesday to Sunday, noon until 7:00 pm.

Further information on Delia Burnham's exhibition *Chemical Landscapes*, downloadable illustrative material, biography and career achievements can be viewed at www.daphneburnham.com.

—30—

APPENDIX F

Public Service Announcements

(Related to the Media Release of appendix E.)

——PUBLIC SERVICE ANNOUNCEMENTS——

(Release Date)
Vancouver, BC
FOR IMMEDIATE RELEASE

Contact: Cindy Chappell
Imagination Gallery
604-555-5555
artpublicists@gmail.com

60-Second PSA

Delia Burnham has non-Hodgkin's lymphoma. During her treatments, she visualizes the fight in her body between the chemicals and the lymphocytes that cause her disease and she has painted her cellular battles. She sees the battles in her mind; her doctors see her battles won on her charts.

This is a celebratory exhibition. Come see how, in vibrant acrylics, the colours of her biochemistry and the contours of her interior landscapes are revealed. This is *not* an exhibition of anatomical or medical details; it is a revelation of the role of the spirit in healing.

The exhibition of Delia Burnham's paintings called, "*Chemical Landscapes,*" opens Wednesday, April 16th at 5:00 pm at the Imagination Gallery, 555 Granville Street in Vancouver. The exhibition runs until Sunday May 18th and is open Wednesday to Sunday, noon until 7:00 pm.

Further information on Delia Burnham's exhibition *Chemical Landscapes*, downloadable illustrative material, biography and career achievements can be viewed at www.daphneburnham.com

— 30 —

30-Second PSA

Delia Burnham has non-Hodgkin's lymphoma. During her treatments, she visualizes the fight in her body between the chemicals and the lymphocytes that cause her disease and she has painted her cellular battles. An exhibition of her painting called, "*Chemical Landscapes,*" opens Wednesday, April 16th at 5:00 pm at the Imagination Gallery, 555 Granville Street in Vancouver. The exhibition runs until Sunday May 18th and is open Wednesday to Sunday, noon until 7:00 pm.

— 30 —

APPENDIX G

Revenue Canada Interpretation Bulletins

Rather than publish the lengthy Canada Revenue Agency Information Bulletins, their updates and interpretation notes, this appendix tells you how to access the information online at the Canada Revenue Agency website. Web site navigation often changes, however, so updates to this process will be posted on the Artist Survival Skills website (www.artistsurvivalskills.com) as will any other information pertaining to taxation and artists.

At the time of publication of this primer, this is how to access the Canada Revenue Agency Interpretation Bulletins.

1. Go to the Canada Revenue Agency website: www.cra-arc.gc.ca
2. In the red box at the top of the page marked, "Search this site" type in "Interpretation Bulletins."
3. You will have been directed to another page listing several numbered options. Look for the link entitled, "Current income tax interpretation bulletins (ITs)" and click on that link.
4. You will be directed to a page that displays, among other resources, "IT-INDEX." Then, depending on what bulletin you wish to read about, do the following:

For Bulletin 504R2, "Reasonable Expectation of Profit"

To see Interpretation Bulletin 504R2, "Reasonable Expectation of Profit" click on the link IT500-IT549. That will open a page with a long list of Interpretation Bulletins. Look down the list and click on the link to "IT504R2-CONSOLID Visual Artists and Writers."

You will then be given viewing options: Choose "PDF it504r2-consolid-e.pdf unless you prefer one of the other options.

For Bulletin IT514 "Work Space in Home Expenses"

To see Interpretation Bulletin 514, "Work Space in Home Expenses," click on the link IT500-IT549. That will open a page with a long list of Interpretation Bulletins. Look down the list and click on the link to "IT514-Work space in home expenses."

You will then be given viewing options: Choose "PDF it514-e.pdf" unless you prefer one of the other options.

For Bulletin IT473R "Inventory Valuation"

To see Interpretation Bulletin 473R, "Inventory Valuation," click on the link IT450-IT499. That will open a page with a long list of Interpretation Bulletins. Look down the list and click on the link to "IT473R-Inventory Valuation."

You will then be given viewing options: Choose "HTML it473r-e.html" unless you prefer one of the other options.

For Bulletin IT525R on "Self Employment"

To see Interpretation Bulletin 525R, "CONSOLID Performing Artists," click on the link IT500-IT549. That will open a page with a long list of Interpretation Bulletins. Look down the list and click on the link to "IT525R- CONSOLID Performing Artists."

You will then be given viewing options: Choose "PDF it525r-colsolid-e.pdf" unless you prefer one of the other options.

Index